Breakout Blueprint

Break*out* Blueprint

How to Find Your Passion,

Take Action,

and Build a Lifestyle Business

Doug Foley

LIONCREST
PUBLISHING

BREAKOUT BLUEPRINT
How to Find Your Passion, Take Action,
and Build a Lifestyle Business

ISBN   978-1-5445-1550-2   *Hardcover*
        978-1-5445-1549-6   *Paperback*
        978-1-5445-1548-9   *Ebook*

Contents

Part 1

Guiding Principles

Introduction

I was at work when I got a phone call that would change my life forever. It was my wife. She was at the doctor for what we expected to be a routine checkup as she neared the end of her pregnancy with our firstborn. She only had six weeks left, and up until this point it had been fairly routine.

The moment I picked up the phone I knew something was wrong. There were some unexpected findings in the ultrasound, and we needed to do more testing.

I sped down the highway with a million thoughts going through my mind. I wasn't sure what to expect when I got to the obstetrician's office. Our doctor tried to assure us that most of the findings were probably "incidental," but the appointment kicked off six weeks of testing, imaging, worry, and stress.

Everyone tells you how much life changes when you have kids, but nothing could have ever prepared us for the pain, frustration, helplessness, and fear that my wife and I endured for those last few weeks of her pregnancy. Our lives had been turned upside down. I had spent the previous nine years of my career focused on making as much money as I could, trying to ascend the corporate ladder. And now, none of that was helpful. No amount of money could make this ordeal easier, nor could it change the fate of our soon-to-be child. It was a wake-up call and it changed my perspective.

Most of us spend the majority of our lives building a life for someone else. We live for the weekends, dread Mondays, and maybe take a couple of vacations each year (if we can afford it). The lucky few who "make it" to the top are rewarded with a fancy VP title and a raise, yet they're burdened with more responsibility, longer hours, direct reports (and the personalities that come with them), and little to no fulfillment. Compounding the pain is the lifestyle creep that comes with those rises to the top. We buy more things, accumulate more debt, and further entrap ourselves in the lifestyle everyone else wants for us.

Slowly but surely, we build our own prison so that we may spend our lives in servitude.

It took that phone call from my wife and six weeks of pain

and uncertainty to realize this. Your life doesn't have to be like that! You do not need to settle for two weeks of vacation, limited income, or living for the weekend. What if I told you that you already have the skills and potential to live life to the fullest every day? That you can shape a life around the things that *matter*—family, loved ones, experiences? That you can have a business and career that works *for* you, and not the other way around?

Those questions led me to create *The Happiness of Pursuit* podcast, where I had one simple goal: to inspire people to find their passion, take action, and build the life of their dreams. What I didn't expect was how much I would learn about life and business, and how they can coexist. Those lessons led me to write this book so that I could share what I experienced, as well as some of the wisdom of my guests. I was fortunate to interview so many interesting people, from solopreneurs working anywhere they wanted to billionaire industry titans changing the world.

After interviewing over 120 entrepreneurs and building two six-figure businesses in under two years, I can tell you that there is more opportunity now than at any other time in human history to create the life you want. Neither your background, your socioeconomic status, nor your education have anything to do with your future.

Take one of my podcast guests, Nikki Bondura. At an early

age, she developed a love for the game of golf, which led her to play golf at Sacramento State. After college, she doubled down on her passion, and upon graduation she created Nikki B Golf, a site where she reviews anything and everything golf, including products, travel, fashion, and fitness. In February 2018, Nikki and her partner Brad Barnes won Golf Channel's first season of Shotmakers, a Topgolf based competition. Not too long after that, she began making regular appearances on The Golf Channel, eventually landing a spot as the cohost of "The School of Golf."

When you follow your passion, you create opportunities to do more of what you love.

This book is your blueprint to escape the typical 9-to-5 and begin to live life on your own terms. What I share in this book are the lessons and principles that I have learned, and that guests on *The Happiness of Pursuit Podcast* have shared with me. This book will teach you how to create time, freedom, and location flexibility, so that you can experience life at an entirely new level. Instead of working for my career, I made my career work for me. I made time for what mattered and did what I couldn't before, like taking my dad to the Masters for his eightieth birthday, going on trips with my wife, achieving unlimited income potential, and meeting some of the most interesting people in the world. And I'm going to show you how you can do the same.

But first, how did I get there?

After six torturous weeks, on March 22, 2014, in a room filled with doctors and nurses, including a team from the NICU, Harper Foley entered this world, a perfectly healthy baby girl. When she heard my voice, she stopped crying and turned her head in my direction.

Her birth was the catalyst that pushed me to launch *The Happiness of Pursuit Podcast*, to change the focus of my agency (at the time, it was my side hustle), and to make very specific career choices so that I could acquire the skills necessary to build the life I wanted and make a massive impact. Over the last ten years, I have been responsible for multiple industry firsts in marketing and advertising, doubled my income thrice, launched two six-figure businesses, and interviewed some of the most impactful entrepreneurs of our time.

Through these experiences I learned what is possible, and now I want to help you discover your own Breakout Blueprint. Chances are if you are reading this book, it is likely because you want out of the typical 9-to-5, you lost your job and don't ever want to have that feeling again, you are fed up with trying to balance being a good mom or dad with doing your job, or you want some additional income to enjoy more of what life has to offer. In any case, you want to take control of your life.

What I share in the *Breakout Blueprint* will give you the mindset and tools you need to start building the life you were meant to live. It will give you the path to creating more time for yourself, for your family, and for doing the things you love. All that I ask is that you be open to the fact that you have a skill that someone will find valuable, no matter how odd that skill is. Because with the right framework, you can turn that into real freedom.

Let's dive in!

Chapter 1

The Breakout Blueprint

There are two scenes in *Office Space*, a classic nineties satire of everyday work life, that are the most accurate depictions of the typical workday.

The first scene happens early in the movie. The main character, Peter Gibbons (played by Ron Livingston), is being chastised by his boss for putting the wrong cover sheet on the TPS reports. The scene is so famous, it is the basis for thousands of memes, T-shirts, and coffee mugs.

The second scene is with Peter Gibbons again, except this time after his awakening. After showing up in the office late wearing flip-flops, he proceeds to filet a fish at his desk—the fish he caught that morning (which is why he was late). He unscrews his cubicle and, with a gentle nudge, kicks the cubicle wall over into the aisle, giving him the perfect window view.

Peter's character resembles so many of us who are chained to the cubicles and forced to put "cover sheets on TPS reports" all day long. Chances are that if you're reading this book, you are fed up with the monotony of unfulfilling paperwork and you are ready to unscrew that wall and kick it over.

Welcome to the Breakout Blueprint! In this chapter, I'm going to show what that freedom looks like and give you a framework that you can apply to your life to take back control. It's a framework I've developed through my journey as an entrepreneur, and my experiences and mistakes have shaped it. I call it the Breakout Blueprint and it's a simple formula you can apply to find meaning in your work:

Breakout Blueprint = (Passion + Expertise) × (Need + Value)

In this book, I'll explore the components of that formula and look at how you can apply the Breakout Blueprint to your life to build a business that works for you.

I've developed this formula through trial and error: it's an encapsulation of my learnings and my mistakes. My journey into entrepreneurship has been a wild one. I spent more than ten years trying to "get rich quick" in an attempt to fast-track life experiences and buy "nice things," while simultaneously trying to follow a traditional career path, mostly to keep my parents happy (something of a curse, being the youngest of eight kids).

The sad part? Rarely can those two ideas coexist.

Throughout my journey, I was an avid listener of podcasts and audiobooks. During one of my long commutes, I came across an interview with Jeff Hoffman on *Inside Quest*. If you're not familiar with Jeff Hoffman, he's a serial entrepreneur who has helped transform industries, created a Grammy-winning album, and advised world leaders on entrepreneurship. In the interview, he shared a story about his view on entrepreneurship and something he calls "Your Golden Purpose," which is "the intersection of 'the thing you're best at,' 'the thing you love,' and 'something the world values.'" I realized after listening to that interview that not only is it possible for us to find jobs or build businesses around what we love, but it's what we're *meant* to do.

It was that lesson that helped me find the term "Ikigai," which literally means "a reason for being." After the awakening I had during my daughter's birth, the concept of "reason for being" really struck me. It forced me to look at life through a new lens, and to find ways to do more of the things I loved in my work and in my life. I wanted more meaningful experiences, and I wanted my work to fulfill me, not just give me a paycheck. More importantly, I wanted to make space for the people that matter in my life—like my daughter—and to give back something of value to the world.

This realization helped me create the formula, Breakout Blueprint = (Passion + Expertise) × (Need + Value). The greater each element is for you, the greater the impact you can make on the world and the more freedom and fulfillment you will find.

1.1. What Holds People Back

For the longest time, people believed the cubicle life was just the way things were. You didn't choose to be Peter Gibbons from *Office Space*—you *had* to be. If you dared to imagine anything different, then, well, people would roll their eyes and laugh you out of the room. You would be a dreamer.

Making matters worse are your self-doubt and limiting beliefs. Those voices in your head are holding you back and preventing you from finding fulfillment and true happiness, saying, "I'm not good enough to do that...," "Nobody would ever pay me to teach them that...," "I've worked so hard to get where I am...I can't throw that away," "What if I fail…," and the worst of them all, "What will my parents think?"

The list of thoughts holding you back could go on forever, but the truth is, those thoughts are not reality. They are just what you tell yourself to settle for the status quo.

Here is a typical story I hear on *The Happiness of Pursuit*:

> "I went to school and graduated top of my class. I got a good job immediately out of school. I was climbing the corporate ladder…and hated every day of my life! I couldn't take it anymore so I quit and built my business doing something I loved—and in the process changed a lot of lives, and now make three times more than I did at my job."

So much of how we judge success in our society is based on where we went to school, our professional designation or job title, and things we want to buy. Those social measurements become our compass, and eventually we fall victim to Peter Gibbons's fate: we end up sitting in a cubicle, wasting away, feeling unfulfilled, undervalued, and living paycheck to paycheck.

This book is going to break that cycle. No longer do you need to waste away, daydreaming about what life could be—or worse, could have been.

The Breakout Blueprint is the system you can use to build the life you were meant to live. There is no limit to what you are capable of once you master it!

1.2. A Lifestyle Business: What It Looks Like in Real Life

When people say you should love what you do every day, it is often misunderstood as turning your hobby into your job. If you look deeper into this, you'll often find the ones who truly love what they do have tied it to a bigger purpose. This enables them to do more of the things they love. I often refer to this kind of career as an impact-driven or lifestyle business.

If you're looking to make your business and job work for you (rather than the other way around), then you're probably looking at building a lifestyle business. This is what the Breakout Blueprint will help you do.

When most people hear the term "lifestyle business," they usually picture something out of Tim Ferriss's *4-Hour Workweek*: working from a beach with a laptop making millions.

For most of us, that's not realistic. And in my experience, building a business is much more than that. Building a business takes work. It's not easy, but when you align your passion and your expertise, you will find that the work *feels* much easier, because in a lifestyle business the work is more fulfilling. A lifestyle business also gives you the opportunity to create more flexibility in your schedule, as well as an unlimited ceiling for earning potential. Many of you reading this will get to earn what you are actually worth, while working less. You'll feel better.

That said, creating a lifestyle business isn't easy. Starting a lifestyle business is different from starting a typical startup: your thought processes and values need to be different. This is where I went wrong multiple times, and I don't want you to make the same mistake. Here are some lessons I've learned from my journey to create a lifestyle business.

1.2.1. It Can't Be about the Money! (Value Is Worth Ten Times More)

After graduating college, I was focused on one thing: making as much money as I could. I was fortunate enough to land a sales job right out of college and began to accumulate a substantial commission well over $75,000. At twenty-three and right out of school, that was a lot of money.

Living well outside my means in the expectation of receiving my commission, I accumulated credit card debt, bought a car I couldn't afford, and took vacations on borrowed money. Then 2008 came and, like many others, the company I was working for went bankrupt. My commission vanished overnight. I was left with a mountain of debt and no way to pay it off. I had borrowed from the future and now it was time to pay up.

I went from aspirations of wealth to desperation and survival. I borrowed more to try and keep up appearances, only to dig a deeper hole. I began to pursue "side hustle" after "side hustle" in search of becoming an overnight millionaire.

I learned the truth the hard way: there is no such thing as an overnight millionaire.

I had a failed apparel company, a hobby blog about hunting and fishing called the *Ultimate Outdoorsman*, and multiple failed attempts at networking marketing, including one selling makeup (yes, from the same guy who had a hunting and fishing blog).

The final straw was an internet marketing scam called "Lawn Chair Millionaire." Between 2008 and 2010, I was trying to teach myself how to code because I wanted to build a better website. I remember sitting in the living room late at night—probably early morning, around 2:00 a.m.; the glow from the fish tank and my computer were the only lights left on in the house—when I saw an ad for something called "How to be a Lawn Chair Millionaire." I clicked the ad and watched the animated video about how people were making millions by putting ads on their website. I transferred the money I had left between cards just to afford the $297 course. You would think that a college graduate would be smart enough to know that with a name like "Lawn Chair Millionaire," it was sure to be a scam. But in 2010, internet marketing was the "fastpass" to success and I was so desperate to get back to the top that I was willing to take whatever legal shortcut could get me there. The Lawn Chair Millionaire was not it.

It wasn't until 2011 when I had a conversation with a good friend about online marketing that I realized I had been chasing the wrong thing.

He and his future wife were struggling to find leads as real estate agents and needed help. Fortunately, those three years of struggle taught me a lot about marketing online. I offered them a few ideas, and they said, "Can we pay you to help us?" I quickly said yes and gave them a quote on the spot. "$375," I said. "I'll do everything for you! SEO, build a website, manage your ads—I can do it all." (One thing to note: when you get your first client you are going to undervalue yourself, even after reading this!)

I realized something important the moment they hired

me: it wasn't about me! It was about how I could use my knowledge to make an impact on their business. This first client was the beginning of Foley Media, my marketing agency. And as my agency grew, I quickly realized that the more value I could provide, the bigger the impact I could make, and the more people would be willing to pay. It was all about value and outcomes.

As you go through this journey, focus on the value you can create for others, and the income will follow.

1.2.2 There Has to Be a Need (or Want)

I'm a longtime fan of *Shark Tank*, the show where would-be entrepreneurs pitch business ideas to a panel of investors called the "Sharks." What makes the show great is when an entrepreneur asks for multiple seven-figure valuations for their company, and they don't have any sales.

Until you have sold something, you don't have a business. I know hearing that stings, but it is the single most important advice someone can give you. Most people will waste time doing things in their business like writing a business plan, market research, forecasts, creating a website, designing business cards, registering a corporation, finding funding. That's all busy work that distracts you from validating your business. The only reason I know is that I made these same mistakes.

I went down that path with a good friend and business partner. We were trying to build an app that would allow prospective student-athletes to create online profiles and connect with coaches to land athletic scholarships. The problem was that we spent so much time researching it that by the time we were ready to build the app, the NCAA had changed their rules and we were no longer allowed to charge student-athletes for an enhanced profile.

We would have been much better off just building a rough version of the app and getting it out there. Success loves speed: the faster you can move to validate your idea and get a paying client, the more likely you are to succeed.

This is why the right half of the Breakout Blueprint is Need + Value. Without both, you do not have a viable business model.

Most of you will start your lifestyle businesses as solopreneurs, and you will need to figure out how to make money quickly. The easiest way to do that is to find out what your particular client niche needs to get to the next level. Then focus on how you can help them do that. This will make all the difference.

Remember: the greater the need, the greater the opportunity.

1.2.3. You Have to Bring an Expertise to the Table

As you embark on your entrepreneurial journey to create a lifestyle business, you do not need to be everything to everyone. In fact, to be successful quickly, you only need to be the right person to a few select people. I remember when I was working with my first client, I was a yes-man. We were working on their website when then they asked, "Can you do SEO for us too? Oh, can you also do Ads?" The problem with saying yes to everything is that you diminish your value and expertise. You become "a jack of all trades, and master of none."

There is a massive difference between expertise and being an expert. For many of you reading this book, you are probably thinking, "I'm not an expert!" But the honest truth is that we all have expertise in something. We just have to get out of our own way in order to realize that the information, education, and life experiences we each have are valuable to a specific audience. In most cases, it is the very thing you take for granted that holds your greatest value.

For example, a friend of mine has been playing guitar for more than fifteen years. He is so good that he can pick up a guitar, ask anyone to name a tune, and he will start playing and nail it perfectly. To me, he is an expert, but if you asked him, he would likely reply, "I'm just good around the campfire. I'm not an expert."

When you have been doing something long enough, you forget that so much of what you do naturally in your day-to-day life is far beyond what a beginner can do. You forget that it is the people looking to get started who are most in need of help, and they are often willing to pay for it.

You don't need to be the best in the world to help someone. You just need to be able to help raise someone up to your level and ask for compensation in return.

1.2.4. Your Passion Is NOT Your Hobby!

Let me repeat this: YOUR PASSION IS NOT YOUR HOBBY.

I want to be incredibly clear on this, because I almost ruined hunting and fishing for myself by turning my hobby into a business. If you choose to make a business out of the thing you do for pleasure, you will destroy it!

My very first venture into online marketing was a blog called *The Ultimate Outdoorsman*. I created it as a way to share my hunting and fishing adventures—plus, I wanted to see how websites were built. I took the time to learn to code, wrote a few posts, had them published on some outdoor sites, and was trying to find a way to monetize it so that I could host my own hunting and fishing TV show. If that happened, I figured I could spend more time hunting and fishing.

Fast-forward three months to the dead of winter when there is no hunting or fishing season open. I ran out of my own adventures to write about. So, I forced myself to create articles to keep the site alive, but what I once loved about the subject was ruined by the mandate to maintain the blog and publishing process. The quality of the articles suffered for it, and what I enjoyed writing about became tedious. It turned into a job.

After six months of struggling and regularly embarrassing myself, I realized something vitally important to building a lifestyle business. The reason I wanted to make so much money was to give myself more time to do the things I loved. I couldn't build a business *in* hunting or fishing, because it would steal from my enjoyment of those hobbies. I had to dig a lot deeper to uncover my true calling. I had to admit to myself that hunting, fishing, and playing golf were not the things I was most passionate about—they were simply things I loved to do in my spare time. That is not to say you can't build a business doing those things. One of my podcast guests, April Vokey, has built an amazing business traveling the world fishing and interviewing other anglers because it is her true passion.

Although it took me a few years to realize it, my true passion, the thing that gave me fulfillment, came from helping people build businesses. It was why I went to school for marketing in the first place. And once I realized that, the question for me became: "*How* do I create more free time to do the things I love?"

When you begin your lifestyle business, remember: you have to base it on your passion, not your hobby.

1.3. The Breakout Blueprint

As you might have noticed, each of my lessons is now an element of the Breakout Blueprint: Value, Need, Expertise, and Passion. But I didn't begin with this formula. So how did I bounce back from my downward spiral as the "Ultimate Outdoorsman"? A lot of learning, and trial and error! When I say a lot, I mean more than ten thousand hours of audiobooks, podcasts, and interviewing people who built lifestyle businesses like the one I aspired to create.

In that same interview between Tom Bilyeu and Jeff Hoffman on *Inside Quest*, where Jeff Hoffman explained the "Golden Purpose," he wrapped up by saying that "entrepreneurship is the shovel we use to dig a path to a brighter future." The moment I heard that quote, I thought, "Holy shit, this is it!" The entire approach I had taken to business was wrong. I was solely focused on what I could do to make money for my own happiness. I had completely missed the goal of being an entrepreneur, which was to leverage my knowledge to help others.

I started to look at the work I was doing for my clients, and I realized that I was most passionate about helping them grow their businesses so they too could live better lives. I was able to do that by using the expertise in marketing I'd gained through years of trial and error and professional experience. Once I had that realization, it became abundantly clear that if I could find more clients who had a similar need and valued my expertise, I could grow my accidental side hustle into a lifestyle business that would give me true freedom.

While it took me over seven years to get from working with my agency's first client to uncovering my personal own Breakout Blueprint, I want this book to be your guide to start your journey to freedom today! I'll begin by finding out what really matters to you in chapter 2. Then, in chapters 3 to 6, I'll dig into the different elements of the Breakout Blueprint; I'll explain the philosophy of each element in depth and you'll see how it applies, in practical terms, to the lifestyle business you want to create. By the end of these chapters, you should have a good idea of what each element means to you—in other words, you should have a Breakout Blueprint of your own.

After that, I'll take the Blueprint to the next level. Chapters 7 to 8 will walk you through the practical steps of setting up a lifestyle business and building your Breakout Blueprint in the real world.

If you don't know what you're passionate about or if you're terrified that you're not "good enough" to charge someone for your services, that's OK! I am going to show you how to uncover those limiting beliefs and find the people who value what you're best at! All you need to know is that you're ready to say goodbye to TPS reports and break the chains on your cubicle. If so, let's dive in.

Chapter 2

Begin with What Really Matters

Growing up as the youngest of eight children, I was fortunate to have a lot of family time. Like most families we had a number of traditions, but one in particular stood out, and that was Friday nights. Every Friday after my family finished work and school, everyone would trickle into my parents' house for pizza. To put it into context, I'm more than twenty years younger than some of my brothers and sisters, so our get-togethers included my nieces and nephews. It was always a full house, and I loved it.

Fridays were never intended to be something formal, there was no set time, and people bounced in and out based on what other plans they had set up to kick off the weekend. When I was in high school my friends would often show up, which was welcomed. It was simple, and great!

Fast forward fifteen years, and two kids of my own...

I had just gotten back from a work trip to Atlanta. As I was getting settled, my daughter said to me, "Hey, Daddy, come into Mommy's room to watch a show..."

I had spent most of my career in sales roles covering the majority of the United States and Canada, which meant a lot of travel. As my roles grew, so did the travel schedule. It reached the point where I was often gone two or three weeks per month, traveling from coast to coast and from north to south. When you are newly married and without kids, this is a great perk because your spouse can tag along on occasion. But when you have two kids under the age of three, it adds an entirely new level of stress.

At first when my daughter said, "Come into Mommy's room," I laughed, but later that night it started to sink in. If I didn't make some changes, it really was going to be *Mommy's* room. Between the travel, running a podcast, and trying to grow my side hustle into a real business, there wasn't a lot of family time left.

I had abandoned one of the fundamental things that makes life great, even as I told myself, "I'm doing this for our family." I was missing the little things. I needed to make a change because the moments I was missing mattered.

I changed my career and refocused on my business to put what matters most, first. My family built new traditions together, and we continue to build upon them today. The first was Friday nights, followed by date nights on Wednesdays. Setting these nonnegotiable events helped me to better understand the lifestyle I wanted and the changes I needed to make for it to become a reality.

The reason I'm putting this chapter here is to stop you from building another job you hate—or worse, from tearing apart the life you're trying to build. In chapter 1, I told you that this book will help you understand your Breakout Blueprint so that you can build a lifestyle business. And it will. But to do that effectively, you have to start with what matters the most. You have to design your life *around* your priorities. Trust me—I learned this the hard way.

2.1. The Entrepreneurship Hustle Mentality

Considering that we spend more than half of our lives in a profession, it's a tragedy that we don't spend more of that time doing what we love. Most of us struggle to get out of bed on Monday, dreading the commute to work and the five days of hell. We live for the weekends.

When I began my journey, my goal was to break out of that rut. Thanks to what I learned from Ikigai and various interviews and podcasts, I began to ask myself the right questions to discover my passion. Over time and after many false starts, I learned that my passion was marketing.

I've been a fan of digital marketing since long before I built my agency. It was the driving force behind the *Ultimate Outdoorsman* blog experiment. I taught myself how to code, which led to a partnership with an online clothing company selling fishing apparel, which forced me to learn how online marketing worked. While those businesses never got off the ground, the lessons they taught me helped me land my first digital marketing client.

It took more than years, but by simply taking action I realized that my true calling was in marketing. I made the conscious decision to find jobs that would give me the opportunity to learn as much as I could, as fast as I could, in order to become one of the best marketers in the industry.

For the next five years, I read every book, listened to every podcast, watched every webinar, and attended every conference I could. I learned ten times more in those five years than I did in school—including powerful life lessons, such as:

If you chase two rabbits, you catch none.

During those five years I also grew my agency, got married, started a family, launched a podcast, and wrote this book...

To say my plate was full was an understatement. I had embraced the "entrepreneurship hustle mentality," but with no direction. I had lost sight of the alignment I had found through Ikigai. I was reverting back to my old habit of chasing money.

My lifestyle business was meant to give me freedom. But instead, I had built a new trap. I was living for the weekends again, except now the weekends were full of even more work and, with two growing kids, way less time.

This chapter is here so that you don't make the same mistake I did. After reading a number of books, including *Essentialism: The Disciplined Pursuit of Less* by Gregory McKeown, *Extreme Ownership: How U.S. Navy SEALs Lead and Win* by Jocko Willink and Leif Babin, and *The One Thing* by Gary Keller and Jay Papasan, I recognized that I was doing the right things, but in the wrong order. I had to ask myself a simple question: "What's the one thing I need to finish or do consistently, to make the other things possible?"

Once I answered that, the next step was as simple as "prioritizing and executing."

2.2. Prioritizing and Executing

Before we dive into building your lifestyle business using the Breakout Blueprint, we're going to start by identifying what matters to you, so that you can design your business around it. Here is the framework you can follow to avoid the chaos I caused and make sure you build a lifestyle business that aligns with what you really care about.

1. *What does your best workday ever look like?*

Wait—my best *workday* ever? Yes. Before we design a lifestyle, we need to figure out how to pay for it, which means you'll have to put in some work. Building a business or finding a fulfilling career is going to unlock more power than you could ever have expected, but it takes effort.

Don't take this step lightly. Be honest with yourself. Most people start this exercise when they're going through a life transition. They find themselves deep in self-help books, doing vision boards, planning their goals, and envisioning their "future life" on a beach, a million-dollar house, a yacht, partying with friends...

It's time to be real. We are NOT planning the best day ever

in your *retirement*. We are building a business, and it's going to be work; we just want that work to be as enjoyable and fulfilling as possible. We are envisioning the best possible workday, not your dream vacation or what you would do with lottery winnings.

In what type of work do you find the most joy? For me, it was helping businesses develop a strategy for growth, which in part was marketing. Anytime I was able to share my expertise with a captive audience, whether that was one-to-one, with a group of thirty, or at a virtual summit with over three hundred people, I felt energized. Knowing that I was making an impact on a business owner's success gave me an overwhelming sense of fulfillment. I got the same fulfillment from writing this book, hoping that it would help you build the life you are looking for.

A good question to ask when doing this exercise is: "What do you love about your current job? What did you love about past jobs?" When I'm talking about the "best workday ever," I mean those moments that bring a grin to your face and evoke overwhelming joy—the ones so good you call your friend, your spouse, and your parents to share how awesome it was. That's what we want to replicate.

2. What's your worst workday ever?

Now repeat the exercise, but for the worst workday ever.

Think about your past jobs: what have you hated? In this step, create a list of tasks or responsibilities that bring that empty feeling to your stomach. Tasks you never want to do again.

Look at the two lists of what you love and what you hate. This is quickly going to help you shape your role in your own company, or—if you choose to be a freelancer—determine the type of work you will need to focus on and, most importantly, the type you will need to avoid.

This is an exercise I would suggest you come back to again and again as your business enters different phases or as you evolve as a freelancer. When you first start, you will have no choice but to do some of those things on the list that you hate. But as you grow you should be able to delegate, delete, or outsource more and more of those tasks and focus on the things that are fulfilling and in your "zone of genius" (more about this in chapter 4).

3. What's realistic?

Now that you have an idea of what your ideal work life is, let's try to fit it in with the lifestyle you want.

Before you can build the life you want, you need to understand the life you *have*. The challenge is to be realistic. As I mentioned before, the purpose of this is to build a lifestyle, not your retirement. If you have kids, it's going to be hard to get rid of some of your responsibilities in life, like taking your kids to school, cooking dinner, attending birthday parties, and so on. The objective is to design a lifestyle within the normal constraints of life and then find a way to balance your newfound dream career or business, the life you want to live, and the things that need to exist from day to day.

To start, create a list of your responsibilities. Which of them are nonnegotiable (for now)? Things like picking up the kids, doing laundry, cooking, cleaning, mowing the lawn. Keep this list handy because I will come back to it, and as you grow, you may be able to hire support to eliminate some of the items on the list.

Next, grab a calendar and schedule the nonnegotiable events happening in the next week. Be detailed in your review. Include things like travel time (to and from work and to pick up the kids), grocery shopping, mowing the lawn, cleaning the house, etc. Do not panic during this step. It's going to look like you have zero time for yourself—and chances are this is true, which is why you are reading this book. One of the single most important things you must do is schedule time with the people you care about the most. Plan and pay for your vacation at the beginning of the year, every year. Schedule and commit to a weekly date night with your spouse or loved one.

Lock in your kids' birthdays. The more disciplined you become with protecting the nonnegotiables and tracking your priorities, the better you can design your life.

Now repeat this exercise for the next month and quarter. While I think having an annual plan is nice for envisioning your future, this exercise is likely one of your first times evaluating and implementing major life changes, and if the early part of 2020 has taught us anything, a lot can change in a moment's notice. I would not recommend going beyond a quarter unless there is a major life event planned, like a wedding, an expected child, retirement, or a dream vacation.

This is where it begins to get exciting. Take that list of responsibilities and mark down one of these three things:

- Delegate
- Delete
- Own

This is a list I learned from *Scaling Up* by Verne Harnish, who is the founder of Entrepreneurs' Organization, the host of multiple Global Business Conferences, and an investor in many startups. In the book, he talks about the simple principle of eliminating tasks that prohibit progress. Things like cleaning your home, mowing your lawn, and even cooking some meals are quick wins. Here are some everyday tasks that are easy and quick to delegate and will allow you to free up time to focus on more important things in life:

- Housekeeping
- Mowing your lawn
- Bookkeeping/accounting
- Meal prep
- Laundry
- Childcare/babysitter

The first thing my wife and I eliminated was cleaning. We decided that hiring a cleaning crew weekly freed up our weekends. The second hire we made was regular childcare, who came weekly so we could go out on a date every Wednesday. (If you're friends with another couple, you could trade off and alternate babysitting responsibilities to save money if needed.)

Time is your most valuable asset, and often most underappreciated. When you change your mindset around the true value of your time, you will begin to make smarter decisions about the things that steal time from what you love to do and the things that help you get closer to your ideal future.

To put time in perspective, here is one of the most powerful stories on the subject from Jesse Itzler's TED talk.

Jesse probably has one of the most well-rounded life resumes. He's been a rapper, an entrepreneur, an author, and is best known as the co-founder of Marquis Jet, one of the largest private jet card companies in the world.

"I thought to myself, my dad only has maybe ten more years to live. If I see him every other Christmas that means I only have five more Christmas with him... Holy shit...I'm only going to see my dad five more times before he dies..."

When you look at life from that perspective, is mowing the lawn or cleaning your home that important when it steals from spending time with those who matter the most?

Take another look at the list of your priorities. How many $10/hour tasks are on your list? While it may feel like a financial burden to start outsourcing elements of your life, think about the opportunity cost of those elements, and how they're robbing you of your future and ideal life.

Pick ONE THING on your list and find someone to outsource it to. In order for this to work, it is important that this outsourced time be *reinvested* in one of the core areas of your life. This could be growing your business, building relationships, spending time with the people you love, or making time for your hobbies. Otherwise, you are just wasting time.

Now that you have an idea of what your ideal work week, your responsibilities, and your nonnegotiables are, we can start to put together a realistic plan for your Breakout Blueprint.

To do that, simply use the steps I shared above to plan your week in advance. (I do this every Sunday evening, but you can find a day that works for you.) Here is a summary of the steps I take each week:

1. Write down my responsibilities in these two categories:
   A. Professional (i.e., any major deadlines, meetings, requirements)
   B. Personal (doctors' appointments, pick-up schedules, kids' activities, etc.)
2. Write down my nonnegotiables:
   A. Date Night
   B. Friday Night Fam-Jam
   C. Important Dates (birthdays, anniversaries, weddings, etc.)
3. Open up my calendar and put in the corresponding dates from steps one and two. (I suggest using a calendar on your phone, so you always have access to it.) Do not forget to add any prep work for major projects or meetings.
4. This part is optional: review the list regularly to see if I can outsource or remove any tasks. The more disci-

plined I become about capturing everything I have to do in a week, the better I am at getting rid of tasks that are unfulfilling and steal from the life I want to live.

As we work through your blueprint you will undoubtedly have ideas and want to rush to things like building a website, or creating a brand, or signing a new client. As an entrepreneur, I'm easily excited by the opportunity to create another business or content platform. I often end up overloading my plate, something my wife can attest to, which works against the entire concept of a lifestyle business. To help with this change, start by looking at your week in advance and writing down the nonnegotiables (including date night and some personal time to do what you really want and enjoy), priorities, and goals. From there you will have a quick glimpse at what space exists for fulfilling new projects and client objectives. The first few times you go through this you will likely underestimate some tasks' duration, while overestimating others. This is an iterative process that you will get better at over time.

The tool I have found most helpful with this process is Michael Hyatt's Full Focus Planner, which you can get at www.fullfocusplanner.com. I will also put links to this and other tools at douglasjfoley.com/book.

Over time, this practice will help you identify the business and life tasks you need to outsource. It is a great way to assess your life at a high level. It tells you when you need to hire and what you need help with at home. Life is always going to be in flux, and your priorities will change with it. Going through this planning process regularly will help you avoid creating a ticking time bomb of stress.

Some of you are probably wondering, where is my Breakout Blueprint? Can't I just skip this exercise and get to making money? Sure, but in six to nine months, you will come back to this chapter and wish you'd completed the exercise. Understanding how to avoid the work you hate and do more of the work you love is the first step toward a more fulfilling life. It's what you start with on your Breakout Blueprint: your passion. And that's what I'll cover in the next chapter.

Part II

Designing *Your* Breakout Blueprint

Chapter 3

Passion—Finding Fulfillment

I was sitting in Tom Bilyeu's living room, about to interview him *for The Happiness of Pursuit*. It had been two years since I started the podcast, and this was going to be the one hundredth episode. I couldn't believe where I was sitting: with Tom Bilyeu!—the founder of the Billion Dollar Brand and Quest Nutrition, as well as the host of *Impact Theory*. He was the person who inspired me to start my podcast. And now I had finally reached episode one hundred—after the craziest two years of my life— and not only was I going to interview someone I had a great deal of respect for, but I was doing it *on* the set of *Impact Theory* and we were doing it *live* on Facebook.

I remember the night before the podcast: going over my notes, rehearsing my questions, trying to shake the nerves. But the morning of the interview, I was surprisingly calm. It was as if I had known that this moment would come—I'd had ninety-nine interviews to practice. When I arrived at Tom's home, I was blown away; the staff were incredibly welcoming and supportive. The moment we sat down and the cameras flicked on, it was a dream come true.

Yet, here's what I remember most clearly from that interview—an answer that changed my life. I ask my guest the same question at the end of each episode of *The Happiness of Pursuit*: "What is one lesson or story you can share with the listeners to inspire them to find happiness in their pursuits?"

Tom's answer blew me away. He said: "A chocolate bar will make you happy temporarily. What I think you're really asking me is, how do you find fulfillment?"

It was the first time I had heard anyone draw a distinction between happiness and fulfillment. And the moment he said it, it reframed so many aspects of my journey—and it will reframe your journey too.

In this chapter, I am going to teach you the difference between happiness and fulfillment, just as Tom taught me. Understanding the difference between happiness and fulfillment is key to understanding passion, especially when it comes to the distinction between a hobby and a true passion. This is how you start doing more of what you love.

3.1. Why Does Passion Matter?

Before we get to the difference between happiness and fulfillment, we need to understand why passion matters—why it's an element of our Breakout Blueprint.

"Go to school, get good grades, find a good job, save 10 percent of every paycheck, spend wisely, and you will retire rich at seventy-five!" This is one of the biggest lies we have been told! When I look at people who are in their seventies, very few of them have the health and endurance to truly live! While they might be checking things off their bucket list, they are limited by their health. Why would you spend fifty years earning money, only to truly live for the last twenty to thirty years? Why not live every day of your life?

Most of you reading this have spent your careers living for weekends, vacations, and the hope that when you retire you can begin to "enjoy life." If someone told you that you were going to watch a movie that's a hundred minutes long and the first fifteen minutes and last fifteen minutes were good, but the seventy minutes in the middle were the same scene over and over, chances are you'd never want to watch that movie. Yet, that's the way we live our lives.

We have allowed society to shape our futures instead of finding and chasing our true callings. Your true calling gives you fuel; it is your *joie de vivre*!

Steve Jobs probably had one of the simplest methods for validating his life daily, which he outlined in his 2005 Stanford Commencement address: "For the past thirty-three years, I have looked in the mirror and asked myself: 'If today were the last day of my life, would I want to do what I'm about to do?' And whenever the answer has been 'No' for too many days in a row, I know I need to change something."

Yet, most of us never have the courage to ask ourselves that question, let alone acknowledge the answer and make a change. Most of us wait for a sign in the form of a life crisis or a mental breakdown. *Or* we wait for someone to make the change for us by firing us or laying us off.

Think about the first day of your most recent job. You probably had a mix of emotions, but mostly felt excited to contribute. For a moment you were passionate about what you were doing. You felt progress, value, and fulfillment. Fast-forward twelve to eighteen months after the honeymoon period has ended. You are back in that same career rut most people struggle through for twenty to thirty years.

This isn't how it should be. We should be waking up excited to live, to do something meaningful and valuable to the world. I am not saying that once you find your passion, life is euphoric. I'm saying that when you make the shift from a job that pays the bills to something you are passionate about, it will change how your brain functions and how you choose to work.

This is why passion is the first piece of the Breakout Blueprint; this is why it matters.

To find your true passion, you first need to understand the difference between fulfillment and happiness.

3.2. The Difference between Happiness and Fulfillment

The reason I chose the name *The Happiness of Pursuit* for my podcast is simple. I believe that if we spend our lives chasing happiness, we will never catch it—it will always be just out of reach. Instead, if we spend our lives doing what we love, we will find happiness and fulfillment in our work.

In order to fully understand the power of finding your

passion, we need to understand how fulfillment brings lasting happiness.

Happiness is actually quite simple. It is a chemical release within your brain, and it happens in response to specific stimuli. When your brain experiences something that you perceive as "happy," it releases one of four chemicals: dopamine, oxytocin, serotonin, or endorphins. While each of these chemicals has its own role in creating happiness, they are also the very same chemicals that trigger sadness, fear, and anxiety.

So how does fulfillment differ?

Fulfillment comes from achievements, like winning a championship or reaching the summit of a mountain. In finding fulfillment, you will consistently trigger the "happiness hormones." This consistent release of chemicals brings more joy than a quick release brought on by temporary stimuli (like eating chocolate).

Let's take a look at two examples. If I eat a chocolate bar right now, I'll be happy while I eat it, and maybe for ten to fifteen minutes afterward. This is an artificial release of the happiness hormones, triggered by the chemicals in sugar. Once the sugar leaves my system, so does the feeling of happiness! If you are on a diet, you may even feel guilt and depression once the euphoria wears off.

Inversely, let's look at someone training for a marathon. For a nonrunner, it can take up to twenty weeks to get ready to run the race. During the first week, they are likely to feel completely miserable and want to give up. By the third or fourth week, they have started to develop a habit of running and their brain is now looking for the happiness hormones in response to this new practice. The runner gets faster and can run longer. Over the course of the twenty weeks they continue to improve. Finally, race day arrives and that person who could barely run a mile twenty weeks ago is about to run 26.2 miles. During the race, they will surely feel fatigued; it is likely that there will be times when they want to give up. But with every step, they will know they are closer to achieving their goal. Eventually, they break through that tape at the end and find fulfillment. And that fulfillment is a lot more than just temporary happiness. It is a memory they can reflect on. When they think about what they accomplished, it will bring a smile to their face.

Lasting happiness comes from the process, not the quick wins. You can find those quick wins by doing the things you love—namely, your hobbies—more often. But it's your passion that will give you the motivation to keep going when the road becomes long and hard; passion is your route to fulfillment.

If you want to build a lasting lifestyle business, you need

to understand the difference between your hobbies and your passion.

3.3. The Difference between a Hobby and a Passion

Growing up, I loved two things: golfing and fishing. From sunrise to sunset, you would either find me on the golf course or by the river. And to be honest, not much has changed other than the locations where I practice these hobbies.

Throughout high school and college, I spent most of my summers working at the golf course. Doing so gave me free membership and access to a practice facility, and I was surrounded by my closest friends who loved the game as much as I did. I was fortunate enough to get a scholarship to a NCAA Division I school, where I got my bachelor's degree in marketing.

Every summer, I would come home from college and people would ask me, "Are you going to turn pro after you graduate?" As I got closer to graduation, I started to look at what a career in golf would look like. Should I double down on improving my game? Should I become a teaching professional? Or should I work as a sales rep for one of the manufacturers, the most realistic option?

Growing up, I saw golf club professionals working late

at the course for very little reward. In my senior year, I had an opportunity to interview for a job as a shoe rep with Titleist, one of the most prominent brands in all of golf. The job was in Iowa, a faraway place where I didn't know a single soul. The final question of the interview was: "Are you willing to relocate to Iowa for the role?" A bit stunned, I replied: "I'm not sure." Not an ideal way to reply in an interview, but hey! At least I was honest. Growing up as the youngest of eight kids, I had always been around family and friends. I hadn't really thought through what it would be like to move to a state where I didn't know anyone.

After the interview, a good friend and early mentor called me to give me some advice. He said: "Doug, the answer to relocating is always 'yes.' Otherwise, it's not your dream job. Working at Titleist is what some people live for."

He was right. Golf wasn't what I wanted to live for. I loved the game, but not as a career. It was a better idea to make a living that allowed me to *play* the game I loved, rather than to build a career that would destroy my love for it!

When you build your lifestyle business based on your Breakout Blueprint, you need to understand that your passion doesn't have to be your hobby. Trying to turn a hobby into a business is one of the fastest ways to ruin something you love. This is because hobbies make you happy—they're the quick wins we talked about above. But they don't give you lasting fulfillment; only your true passion can do that.

Let's revisit the example of Jeff Hoffman, whom I introduced in chapter 1. I interviewed Jeff on episode forty-two of *The Happiness of Pursuit*. I asked him why he chose to become an entrepreneur and what he was most passionate about. His answers surprised me.

Early on in Jeff's career he had always dreamed of visiting every country in the world, but it just seemed as if that dream wasn't happening. One day, he was in the elevator of his office building, headed to the fourth floor where he worked. One of his friends from work got into the elevator and proceeded to push the sixth-floor button. When Jeff got to his desk, he realized he had yet to go up to the sixth floor to visit his friend.

This was his wake-up call. He thought: "If I can't even get to the sixth floor to see my friend, how am I going to see the world?"

The incident fueled his determination. Jeff became so intent on seeing the world that it became the centerpiece of many of his businesses. If you pull back the covers of what he has done, you can see how travel is at the core:

- He helped launch Priceline.com, which you have likely seen advertised with comedian and Star Trek pioneer, William Shatner.
- He invented the technology that allows you to print boarding passes at the airport.
- He founded "Unreasonable at Sea," a philanthropic group that sends a cruise ship of millennials to observe and solve problems around the globe.

Jeff's passion is travel. It took an elevator incident to make him see that he needed to act on it, but once he did, he was able to channel his passion into his businesses. He weathered all the ups and downs and roadblocks, and he stuck to his goals. This is because travel gave him fulfillment—it wasn't a hobby or a quick win. It really mattered to him. And because it did, he was able to build a life around what he loved and change the world in the process.

3.4. Finding Your Passion

So, how can you find your passion and start to change the world on your own terms? Here are five simple questions that can help you find your passion in less than twenty minutes:

- What do you read?
- What do you watch?

- What do you talk about?
- What do you write about?
- What would you do if you knew you couldn't fail?

How To Find Your Passion
look at What You love

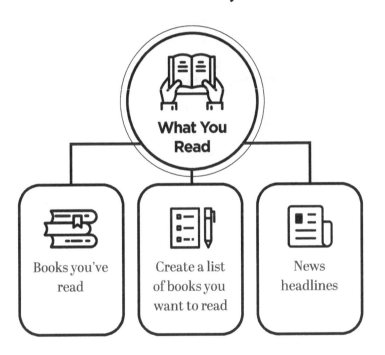

What You Read

Books you've read

Create a list of books you want to read

News headlines

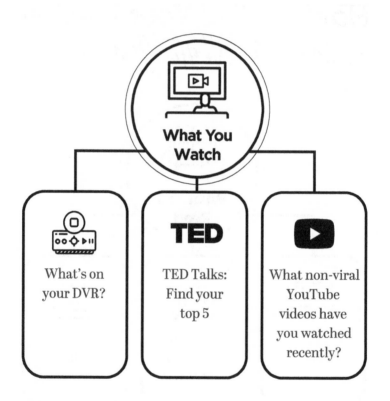

What You Talk About

- At work
- At play
- With those closest to you
- With someone you meet for the first time

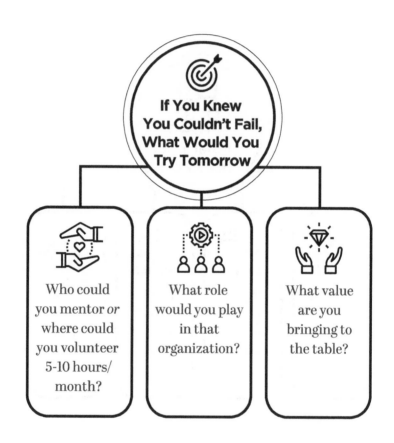

If You Knew You Couldn't Fail, What Would You Try Tomorrow

Who could you mentor *or* where could you volunteer 5-10 hours/month?

What role would you play in that organization?

What value are you bringing to the table?

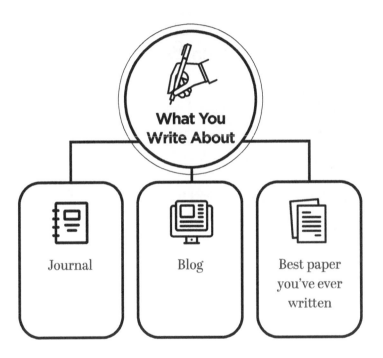

What You Write About

Journal

Blog

Best paper you've ever written

Bring It All Together

Read through your responses
and look for trends. What are the overlapping
areas of interest? Google some of them and see what blogs
get your attention. Chances are someone
has created a business in a similar niche industry.

Once you answer these questions, analyze your answers. What trends do you see? Make a list of common themes and industries of interest. By consciously observing yourself and your habits, you can uncover your true passions. Think of the last book you read. What did you do with the information you learned from it? Did you share it with someone to help them solve a problem?

It took me almost seven years to realize that nearly every book I read was about one of two things: marketing / business growth and personal development. I started to notice that I was always sharing what I learned from these books with business owners and other marketers. When I was able to help them put it into practice, they saw results—this is what lit the fire in my belly!

It is highly unlikely that immediately after finishing this chapter, you will be able to identify your true passion. Remember, it took me over seven years to get to where I am today, and I am constantly making adjustments to better understand who I am. But reflecting on your interests is an important step toward getting to know yourself better, and it will make a massive impact on your Breakout Blueprint.

By following the steps in this chapter, you can focus your time and energy on the things that provide the greatest fulfillment. This is the first step to unlocking your true passion, which will give you the superpower you need to start a massively successful business.

If you want a fillable PDF of the steps we talked about in this chapter, you can grab that at douglasjfoley.com/book.

In the next chapter, I'll combine the steps to finding your passion with your expertise to complete the first half of your Breakout Blueprint. Now that I've show you why passion matters and how placing true passion at the center of your business can lead to fulfillment, I am going to show you how to master your passion and create massive value for people. Think of it this way: Jeff could have settled for life as a travel agent and likely found a way to visit every country in the world, but instead he used his passion to fuel a business that changed lives, provided fulfillment, and enabled him to travel the world as a guest of world leaders.

Chapter 4

Expertise—Your "Zone of Genius"

One out of every ten small businesses fails. Many failed entrepreneurs make excuses: lack of access to capital, lack of access to talent, or simply bad luck. But the honest truth? They weren't good enough.

After doing one hundred interviews on *The Happiness of Pursuit*, I realized something profound: each of the unique entrepreneurs I'd spoken with pursued a level of mastery. This ranged from reading classic literature for Audible, to revolutionizing travel, to fulfilling childhood dreams of being on the Golf Channel. In each case, their dreams came true because they weren't just good—they became great.

Remember the Breakout Blueprint: (Passion + Expertise) × (Need + Value). I've covered passion in the last chapter, and there's a reason it's linked to expertise. In order to have a truly successful lifestyle business, you need to work harder than ever before to master what you love. Businesses survive and succeed when the people running them have developed their skills to a higher level—they have become masters of their craft, which is why they consistently rise above their competition.

It took me a while to understand this. Growing up, I was surrounded by entrepreneurs. My grandmother owned a flower shop, my grandfather owned his own painting business, my father owned a woodshop, and my brothers owned sunglass shops, engineering firms, and a store fixture company. To say entrepreneurship was in our blood would be an understatement. But my path through entrepreneurship involved as many identity crises as it did life lessons.

In 2014, I was trying to make it big selling makeup as part of a network marketing company. I was sold on the opportunity because I saw my chance to "level up" and get a white Mercedes. I was so fixed on the end results that I didn't focus on the value I could bring to my clients; I wasn't focusing on my passion and I definitely wasn't playing to my strengths. I had absolutely no talent for selling makeup. Other than the time my sisters accosted me when I was three years old, I had never had a single shade of eyeshadow on my face.

Within four months, I had failed. I didn't have the motivation, nor could I get past the embarrassment of admitting what I was doing. I was chasing the "shiny object"—the white Mercedes—not the area where I could provide the most value. It wasn't the company's fault; they gave me support materials, coaching, and a formula for success. It was and is an incredible company for the right people. The problem was simply that I wasn't good enough, and I lacked the passion and expertise to change that.

It wasn't until three years later that I realized my true calling was in helping small businesses compete and I doubled down on my expertise in digital marketing to build Foley Media. Looking back at my own failures and successes, I can now honestly say that every time I failed, it was because I wasn't good enough. In this chapter, I am going to help you uncover your true expertise so that you don't make the same mistakes I did.

4.1. Zone of Genius

As of my writing this book, Foley Media has doubled in size every year for the past three years and it is because of one simple thing: I found what Gay Hendricks identified as the "zone of genius."

This was summarized in a *Forbes* article by Brianna Wiest in September 2018: "In this zone, you capitalize on your natural abilities which are innate, rather than learned. This is the state in which you get into 'flow,' find ceaseless inspiration, and seem to not only come up with work that is distinguished and unique, but also do so in a way that excels far and beyond what anyone else is doing."

I was able to slip into the zone of genius with Foley Media because the organization was at the intersection of my passion and my expertise. I found what I was good at— the thing I wanted to be better at than anyone else! I wanted to become the master. The more clients I helped, the more I learned. The more I learned, the more value I could bring back to clients. The more value I brought, the higher my rates. I spent hours reading, researching, attending conferences, networking with people ten times better than me. I charted my career path to expose myself to specific opportunities to learn from the best.

To put this mastery into perspective, let's consider a familiar situation: going to the doctor. For this example, I'll use going to the doctor because it's something we're all familiar with.

At the onset of symptoms, you make an appointment. Your next step is usually going to see your doctor, who is most likely a general practitioner (or nurse practitioner). They will do their assessment, and if it is severe enough, they'll send you to get an x-ray, which is performed by an x-ray technician, who specializes in body imaging. They then send the report to the radiologist, who reviews the documents and determines the severity of your infection. If it is bad enough, you are then sent to the surgeon for surgery.

As you can see, as you ascend through the process, you start working with people who have more training and expertise. People are often rewarded for their expertise for one simple reason: their advice and decisions have greater consequences. If the general practitioner misdiagnoses your condition, you will likely return in twenty-four to forty-eight hours. If the surgeon makes a mistake, you could die.

The reason I want you to understand this framework is that it will help you decide what type of work you are going to do. In practical terms, this directly relates to what you are going to charge. The higher the degree of expertise (and mastery), the higher the value to your customer, and the higher you can charge.

But before we can figure that out, we need to deal with one of the biggest things that holds entrepreneurs back: imposter syndrome.

4.2. Dealing with Imposter Syndrome

Whether you're just getting started or you're well on your

way to building your dream business, you will inevitably come face-to-face with doubt. You will doubt your idea. You will doubt your customers. Most importantly, at some point, you are going to doubt yourself.

Almost every entrepreneur I have interviewed experiences the fear that they're not good enough. The difference between the entrepreneurs you see on the cover of *Forbes* and everyone else is that the cover-story entrepreneurs kept learning. They pursued a level of mastery far beyond that of their peers and competitors, and in doing so, they destroyed any fear of not being good enough.

This is no different than the way Michael Jordan worked his ass off to become the best player in the NBA's history.

Right now, you're probably thinking: "That's great—I went to college for four years, got my master's, and now you're telling me I need to learn something totally new all over again?"

Not at all. Quite often it is the hidden talents beyond your traditional schooling that you are more likely to master and profit from.

That is exactly what Jen Berson did when she left her law career to launch a PR agency.

When I first interviewed Jen in 2015, she was approaching the ten-year mark with her PR agency. The interesting thing about Jen's story is that she was not professionally trained in PR. In fact, she had a very successful law career as a civil litigator in Los Angeles before she started pursuing her passion for beauty, baby, and lifestyle brands.

She became a student of the subject, learned quickly, and steadily grew her agency and her reputation. By the time I interviewed Jen a second time two years later, she had tripled her business and was in the process of launching Jeneration Academy, an online educational platform for entrepreneurs.

Since then, Jen's PR agency and online education platform have continued to take off.

This is proof that when you focus on developing an expertise and work hard, you can build whatever you want.

So, the question for you is: "What are you great at and what are you willing to go all in to get better at?"

4.3. Finding Your Expertise

To find out what you are good at, all you have to do is ask.

Here's a simple piece of advice from *New York Times* best-selling author Keith Ferrazzi, who wrote *Never Eat Alone* and *Who's Got Your Back*:

"Call, text, or email at least ten people and ask, 'What is the one thing in the world you think I'm best at?'"

When I first heard this, I was doubtful. I thought to myself, "It can't really be that easy." I sat on the advice for about three months, in fear of what people would really say for two reasons:

1. I was afraid that what I thought of myself was wrong.
2. I was afraid that they would say what I thought, and then I would be forced to act on it.

I emailed past colleagues, friends, classmates, clients, and even a couple of professors. It had been ten years since I graduated and I had lost touch with some of the contacts, but something weird happened—they all came back with similar answers.

All of the replies centered around marketing, communications, and small business. One of the replies even said: "I thought you would be running your own agency by now, not working for someone else."

Asking people what I was best at put me in a position where I had to act. But I still needed a little bit of help.

Fortunately, throughout my life, I have learned from a number of mentors, one of whom is Paul Edwards. We met as opponents during a doubles match at our home golf course in Ontario, Canada, the first of many rounds we've played together. Most of our rounds have involved me asking for advice or referrals, which he has gladly helped with, but one day he surprised me with a profound statement, "Foley, if you don't go build this agency now, I will kick your ass." I was a little shocked, but he went on to explain, "The longer you wait to do this, the harder it is going to get." He was right. If I waited to build my dream, I would likely get too comfortable in a traditional corporate job to take the leap necessary. To this day, I will never forget that round with Paul. It was the catalyst for doing what I'm doing today.

After that subtle kick in the ass, I had a new sense of direction. I looked at the leaders in the marketing industry and at other business models. I came to the conclusion that I needed to make a career change to better hone my skills. I put myself in a position to learn from true masters of the craft—some of the best marketers in the world. I found a job that gave me access to the top marketing conferences in North America and learned as much as I could from the best of the best.

The more I learned, the more knowledge I craved—that is how I knew I was on the right path. I was developing my "zone of genius," and the work never bothered me. I became a constant student and practitioner of marketing. This passion for learning and mastering a skill is what sets high performers apart.

I looked for jobs that gave me opportunities to learn and hone my "zone of genius." Changing jobs on an annual basis was a bold and unconventional decision, but I knew that if I could understand how things worked in different industries and roles, I would be better prepared when it came time for me to run my own agency. I want to be clear: I was very intentional with each role I chose and knew how I wanted each one to enhance my skills as a marketer. I am not suggesting you job hop; I knew my end goal very early and was willing to put in the time to get there.

When you combine your passion, knowledge, and skillset with that thirst for mastery, you have the foundation for a fulfilling and rewarding business that will provide so much value, customers will be begging to work with you. *That's* what you should be aiming for.

Now that I've shown you how passion and expertise can come together to create something unstoppable, let's move on to the next element of the Breakout Blueprint: need. In the next chapter, I'll explore the foundation you need to establish to start your long-lasting lifestyle business.

Chapter 5

Need—What Problem Can You Solve and for Whom?

I started Foley Media by accident. A good friend of mine asked a few questions about digital marketing, which at the time was primarily SEO and the beginning of content marketing. We met a few weeks after the initial conversation, and I put together a strategy and a monthly retainer to help them find more customers.

See, the interesting thing for them was that they knew they were missing out on attracting clients online and that, in order to grow, they had to get into this space. I happened to have the knowledge to get them there. I didn't have a business plan, a website, or business cards. I simply knew how to fix their problem.

By the end of this chapter, you should be able to identify three to five core products or services you could sell within thirty days. This is the next part of our Breakout Blueprint: (Need + Value). This chapter will tackle "need"—that is, is there demand for your services in the market? Can you sell your product and skills? How do you identify which of your skills the market needs?

"If you want to make a billion dollars, try solving a problem for a billion people."

—PETER DIAMANDIS

5.1. Reverse Engineering

So you want to start a business. Where do you begin? Some people start with a business plan or a marketing plan—a brand, a website, business cards. Some even launch straight into hunting for their first clients without knowing what service they're providing. Some design the product or course they're interested in making, with no thought for the market. Don't do any of these things. I have seen far too many clients build their product, service, and online course, only to target it to a market who didn't value it and leave thinking they failed.

Instead, identify "need." This is the single most important thing. Reverse engineer your business by finding the most painful problems in a particular industry or sector and then using your expertise to find unique solutions. In other words, find the problems you can solve. Do NOT try to find your clients first. It is much easier to first find problems you can solve, then look for the industries and customers who will value your solutions.

5.2. What Problem Can You Solve and for Whom?

It doesn't matter if you're trying to build a lifestyle business or the next Uber. If you understand the problems you can solve and the audience who values your solutions, you have the potential to build a profitable business.

So, how do you find the right problem? In most cases, you need to scratch your own itch. Find the problems that you recently solved for yourself, and ask, "Would someone else be willing to pay for that?"

Now let's break down this process, which can take less than an hour.

5.2.1. Scratching Your Own Itch

One of the best ways to find solutions to common problems is to start with your own problems. To do this, download the Brainstorming Worksheet at douglasjfoley. com/book. You can either download it as an Excel file, or copy it to your Google Drive.

If you wanted to build a brainstorming sheet from scratch, here is what I would recommend. Start by creating a Google spreadsheet (I suggest creating this in Google Sheets so that you can access it from your phone whenever an idea strikes you) and adding five columns with the following headings:

- Problem
- FAQ (frequently asked questions)
- Solutions (product/service)
- Need
- Willingness to Pay (value)

To start, simply begin writing down your problems or problems you have seen under "problems." Next, write down some of the solutions you've come up with on your own. Beside that, write down what "need" your solutions address; this will start to form the basis for your product or service. Once the list includes ten to twelve problems, we are going to validate them using some free search tools.

This process works best when you do it regularly because it helps you become more aware of opportunities, especially as you begin to lock in on a particular idea. You will start seeing the real problems, not just what appears on the surface.

As I shared previously, I started Foley Media by accident, but as we started to grow we noticed something. Businesses often came to us to "fix their SEO" or "help rank on Google," but that wasn't the problem they really wanted to solve. They wanted more sales—it just so happened that they believed that if they ranked on Google, more people would visit their website, which would mean more leads. The real problem they were trying to solve was how to get more sales via the internet. The challenge for Foley Media was to get clients to purchase full-service packages and not just SEO (search engine optimization). With that knowledge, we built new solutions for problems at each stage of the client relationship.

To start, we created a video called "SEO is dead" to help answer the initial question of "how to get ranked on Google." At the end of that video, we had a link to book a call to discuss what to do instead.

During our one-hour call with a potential customer, we showed business owners how marketing really works and why SEO is just one of many things that businesses need to implement to compete online. The most important step for businesses is, in fact, to develop a strategy.

Once the potential customer was aware that the problem was the *lack of strategy,* we offered to conduct a paid half-day or full-day strategy session with the business and their team. In most cases, the clients would end up in a full-service or strategy project with Foley Media. This funnel (which is the marketing term for a customer journey) is still in place today and helped us double our revenue three years in a row.

When you focus on solving the right problems in the right order, it is much easier to create a profitable and scalable business.

While this process took me years to figure out and a lot of trial and error, I have adapted it to create the Brainstorming Worksheet so that you can get a head start in understanding the right problems to solve as you build your Breakout Blueprint.

5.2.2. What Does the Market Want to Know?

After completing your brainstorming worksheet, we are going to turn the list of ten to twelve problems you solved into a series of questions to verify the demand and gain intel on your competition. Before you begin, you need to understand three important questions:

- What are your customers' most frequently asked questions?
- What steps can your customers follow to solve a common problem?

- What questions should your customers be asking to avoid the pain/problem in the first place?

We are going to use some quick search methods to research some of your problems and solutions. You can either continue using the Brainstorming Worksheet, or add to the worksheet you created with the following headings:

- Search Volume
- Competitors
- Video Content Links
- Notes

The first step is to reframe a problem you identified as a phrase that is searchable online. For example, if the problem is "getting ranked on Google" you will likely see questions like "How does SEO work?" or "How to get leads online?" If I simply go to Google and enter those questions, there will be about 685,000,000 results. Add that to your list under the new heading "search volume." If you scroll down, you will likely see a number of blog posts, which can give you great insights into your competition. Browse through these and see if any give you new content ideas. Figure out what other questions or problems your customers might have, and what products or services already exist.

Pay close attention to your potential competitors. Browse through their websites and look at the products and services they offer. Sign up for their newsletters and take note of their frequency and their offers—learn how your competitors acquire customers. This will be super helpful as your business grows.

More often than not, it is easier to build a better mousetrap than to start from scratch. Add the links to your competitors' content and videos, as well as any notes you may have, in the columns "video content links" and "notes." Continue to update your Brainstorming Worksheet until you can identify a pattern in the problems that potential customers have. Once you have three to five ideas you want to take to market, you will need to validate if any of them is something clients would pay for.

If you get stuck or have trouble coming up with ideas, here are a few additional resources to try. These tools will give you insight into the questions and problems people really deal with. You can use this research to validate your idea and develop future content ideas:

- Answer the Public (https://answerthepublic.com/)
- Google Trends (https://trends.google.com/trends/?geo=US)
- YouTube (https://www.youtube.com/)
- Quora (https://www.quora.com/)

- LinkedIn (https://www.linkedin.com/)
- Facebook (https://www.facebook.com/)

5.2.3. Competition Is Not a Bad Thing

Do not look at competition as a bad thing. It is a sign of a need in the market. When I built Foley Media, there were thousands of marketing agencies, and that list keeps growing because the market needs marketers.

According to research from Statista.com, "In 2017, there were 13,800 advertising agencies in the US...and 30.4 million small businesses."

That works out to approximately two thousand customers (i.e., small businesses) for each agency. While not every one of those small businesses will advertise, if even a small percentage does, there will be plenty of business to be shared. Competition should not scare you off from an opportunity.

5.2.4. Will the Market Pay for It?

Now that you have some business ideas, you need to confirm there is a market willing to pay for at least one of them.

Once you have ten to fifteen product or service ideas, go

back to the blog posts and competitor links on your worksheet. Look closely at what they offer. Notice how the companies guide you through their funnels with offers, email sequences, etc. If they have prices, even better.

Go back into Google and type in your product or service. See who else comes up. Pay close attention to the ads. It typically signals significant demand and value if companies are willing to pay for the attention of a given audience.

More often than not, especially in the case of online consultants or digital courses, you will need to go through their funnel to see their products, prices, and messaging sequences. Go through these! Not only will you get a backstage pass to their business, but you will also learn something in the process—just don't get stuck buying twenty digital courses and doing nothing with them.

Identifying what the market needs and building a product or service that fills that need is the single easiest way to create a lifestyle business that lasts and scales. In this chapter, I've given you the tools to identify three to five core product or service ideas that will be the foundation of your lifestyle business. In the next chapter, I am going to show you how to validate your ideas and move toward your first sale (all without a business plan). I'm on the last element of the Breakout Blueprint now: value. And that means it's time to figure out what people will pay for.

Chapter 6

Value—What Gets You Money

Over the course of my career, I have had so many failures: from network marketing to an app to an online apparel company. The one thing consistent across each of these failures? I built the product first and tried to sell it second.

A kid who cuts grass in the summer doesn't need a website or business cards to launch their business—they just need to know people with long grass and to have the courage to ask if they can cut it.

There are many articles about people like me, who seem to be "born entrepreneurs," as if it were in their DNA. Being an entrepreneur doesn't mean you had to grow up buying and selling baseball cards like Gary Vaynerchuk.

It doesn't mean having a paper route or launching some hot startup in your twenties.

It's much easier than that. In fact, it is one of the easiest business lessons to learn:

- Find a problem.
- Solve it.
- Be willing to ask for compensation.

If you can master those three things, then the rest comes down to understanding the value of your solution to your customers' problem. The greater the pain or problem, the greater the value of the solution.

In this chapter, I am going to show you how to avoid the mistakes most *wantrepreneurs* make when building a business—the mistakes that explain why most small businesses fail. This is the final piece of the Breakout Blueprint: value. Understanding the value of your solution is crucial, because it directly connects to how much money you will make. The more valuable your solution is, the more money your clients will be willing to pay. In this chapter, I'll tackle value in practical terms: I'll list the possible lifestyle businesses you can create to offer the most value to your clients, and then I'll tell you how to go about starting those businesses. I will give you exactly what you need to find your first customer and then grow.

6.1. Types of Lifestyle Businesses

When it comes to building a lifestyle business, it is much easier to create time and financial freedom by monetizing your expertise than it is to build out a product-based business. I am going to walk you through four different kinds of knowledge-based or skill-based businesses. This is not to say you cannot build a product-based business as a lifestyle business; it just requires more time and significantly more risk.

The primary lifestyle businesses:

- Online Training
- In-Person Training/Services
- Freelance Gigs (Skill Specific)
- Coaching and Consulting

6.2. Online Training

Online coaching has seen explosive growth over the last ten years. So much so that your Instagram feed is polluted with coaches selling online training programs about how to build and launch an online training program.

It's not too late to get into the game, but there are a few things you need to know if you plan to go down this path. Most importantly, it has become a pay-to-play sport. Unless you have created a ton of content, you have a large audience and email list, or you are a celebrity, you will have to advertise to get your course seen. With the rising costs on Facebook and other platforms, unless you are selling a course over $1,500, it has become increasingly challenging to make money doing this.

If you want to go down this road, I would encourage you to look at destinations that already have a captive audience until you have enough momentum to market the course on your own. Two of my favorite platforms for this are Teachable and Udemy.

The other thing to note about building your online course is the level of technical expertise and time required to create high-quality audiovisual content and the supporting materials that go with them.

I want to dispel one of the most pervasive myths about online courses: there is no such thing as "passive income." Online courses are a product and require constant promotion. The moment you take your foot off the gas, your business slows down. As ad costs continue to rise, it becomes harder and harder to maintain profitable funnels.

If you do decide that this is a path you want to pursue, I have compiled a list of the resources and programs that helped with my growth, including our flagship program.

These resources, which I have personally invested in, are available at douglasjfoley.com/book.

6.3. In-Person Training/Services

In-person training has tremendous potential. From sales training to yoga instruction, you have an opportunity to share your passion and expertise in a variety of settings. Depending on the type of training you choose, there can be both opportunities and challenges with in-person training, most notably in regard to location.

For example, a yoga instructor in San Diego can host twenty people or more in a local park almost any day of the year. A sales trainer in Minneapolis in the dead of winter likely has to source a space to accommodate his audience.

The important thing to remember when going down this path is to think through the delivery of your training with these four questions:

1. Who am I training?
2. Where am I training them?
3. How will I deliver the training?
4. How much do I charge?

As you think through these questions, look back at your

Brainstorming Worksheet from the previous chapter. Think about the problem you are solving, and how training can bring your solution to life. Remember, value goes hand in hand with need in the Breakout Blueprint; they're intertwined.

To make this process easier to grasp, let's use the example of a personal chef. Imagine that as a personal chef, you have identified that the parents you work for are too busy to cook good meals for their families of four. Their kids are picky eaters and need to eat before they get "hangry." You have around twenty meals that are fun to make and that you can prepare and cook in less than thirty minutes. Now, you just need to figure out how to get people to your training.

Who am I training?

Fortunately, there are a number of ways you can offer your program. Option 1 is to start a "cooking class" at a local culinary studio or country club and invite one or both of the parents to participate in a group setting. Option 2 is to do one-on-one home training with families.

Where am I training them?

To help make the choice, let's look at both options from the previous answer in more detail.

Option 1 requires you to find a host and/or venue. If you are going down this route, it is worthwhile to partner with some vendors and figure out how to exchange services or establish a revenue share with them.

Option 2 simply requires you to show up with the groceries and likely some sharp knives (there's nothing worse than trying to prepare a meal with a dull kitchen knife).

The difference comes back to finding quick wins. This is not to say you should always take the easy way out, but understand that when you are starting your business, it is important to find where you can provide your ideal customer with the biggest value in the shortest amount of time.

If you master Option 2, it will be much easier to leverage your customers' referrals and build a loyal audience to fill your first large event. If you already have a following and solid reputation, you may be able to dive right in and offer cooking classes right out of the gate. Just build the business for where you are and who you can help.

How will I deliver my training?

Your delivery should match your personality. If you hate talking in front of large groups of people, don't start there! Find more intimate settings where you can be yourself. Eventually, if you want to scale in-person training, you will need to get comfortable with larger audiences, but you do not need to *start* there.

This is one of the rare situations in which I will tell you that you do not have to get comfortable with being uncomfortable. You need to be comfortable enough to deliver great training. If the size of the crowd is distracting you from the skill you are transferring, scale it back!

The other thing to note with delivery is compensation. The more exclusive the training, the more likely someone is to value the attention and pay you. If I had someone in my home teaching my family how to prepare easy-to-cook meals, I would expect to pay more than restaurant prices; for a class with twenty people, I'd expect to pay less.

How much do I charge?

Quick tip for income goals from Tim Ferriss: if you want to quickly understand what to charge per hour, simply take the income goal and divide it by two thousand. Be cognizant of your income goals when you price things hourly, because for most in-person training opportunities, you will not be able to work a full forty-hour week (which is what the above calculation is based on). Plus, you may only want to work 30 percent of the time. In which case, you can simply adjust as follows...

$50/hour divided by the percentage you want to work (in this case 30 percent) = $50/0.3 = $166/hour.

Each private cooking class for a family of four will likely take two hours of instruction, plus one hour of meal planning and grocery shopping. Therefore, $166 × 3 = $500 for a cooking class. You can adjust that up or down to suit your market, but remember, you are only as valuable as what you are willing to accept as payment.

Examples of in-person training/services:

- Yoga classes
- Cooking classes
- Personal training
- Massage
- Naturopathy
- Sales and marketing training
- Photography

How do I find clients for in-person trainings?

Here are a few examples of where to find clients. For yoga, personal training, and massages, start with existing businesses. Look for institutions like golf courses, gyms, tennis clubs, or other athletic facilities your ideal clients are likely to frequent. You can also look for organizations and/or businesses that may be looking for ways to improve their culture.

If your coaching is related to a sport or activity, look for programs or associations that specialize in that sport/ activity and would benefit from your expertise.

If your coaching is related to sales or marketing, pick an industry and look on LinkedIn for people responsible for scheduling the training in that industry. If you train sales people who specialize in "at-home sales," look up the regional sales managers of five to ten companies in the area that have salespeople doing home visits, like window contractors, roofing companies, mobile mortgage brokers, and other home service companies.

One thing I have learned from personal experience about doing prospect: if you are selling a higher-ticket service (something that costs more than it would cost a company to hire someone internally for), try to focus on companies selling more expensive products or services. For example, consider the difference between roofing companies and lawn-care companies. One roof might cost $8,000 to $30,000, where as a lawn-care contract might be $2,500. The value of the results you can deliver is much higher for the roofing company, and they can see a return much faster.

6.4. Freelance Gigs (Skill Specific)

As a result of COVID-19, more people than ever before have figured out how to work from home. This has opened up the opportunity for people to find independent projects or "gigs." In the simplest terms, this means that specialists are leaving businesses to work as freelancers performing specific tasks such as web development, graphic design, or copywriting. Rather than have this talent in-house, businesses can call upon these individuals when needed.

The gig economy has benefits for both parties. From a business owner's perspective, the money that would have been a full-time specialist's salary can be redirected to another job or project. And the freelancer likely gets paid more per hour than they would if they were an employee.

Being a freelancer is also a great way to turn your "side hustle" into a business, where you yourself begin to hire freelancers and contractors to fulfill client work. This is the point I have reached with Foley Media. Depending on what you want your lifestyle business to look like, this may be a great business model for you.

Freelancers commonly perform creative tasks that do not require a physical presence during the workday. This business model best suits graphic designers, website developers/coders, copywriters, data analysts, virtual assistants, bookkeepers, etc.

How do I find work as a freelancer?

There are a number of websites that allow you to bid on freelance work. However, you often end up in a race to the bottom and spend a lot of time bidding on projects that are hard to win. Most of the websites that offer freelance work are heavily dominated by foreign workers who are willing to work for less and have driven down the costs.

When you first start, it is best to network among your family and friends. In chapter 7, I will give you the exact scripts to use when you are ready to prospect for a new business. It will be important for you to develop a portfolio to showcase your expertise. When it comes to creative work, clients will inevitably want to see your work before hiring you as a freelancer.

In certain cases, you may want to work with a partner (i.e., an agency) on a trial basis to build your portfolio and reputation. If you do this, make sure you limit your trial time, so that partners or early clients do not take advantage of your talents. Remember, I charged only $375/month for my first client. It's not a mistake you should repeat.

6.5. Coaching and Consulting

Consulting used to be considered the place where "careers go to die." But as companies and industries have evolved, there has been a growing need for true experts who understand complex problems. As with creative freelancers, it is often more beneficial for companies to outsource this need than to hire someone full-time. A lot of companies are hiring people on consulting contracts as a means to "try before they buy."

Coaches and consultants charge anywhere from $50 to $5,000 per hour. Some charge even more. Why such a big range? Because a consultant's fee is directly related to the value and impact of their expertise.

The biggest difference between freelancers and consultants/coaches has to do with outcome. With freelancers, companies are usually hiring for a specific skill that relates to a project, whereas they hire a coach or consultant for their expertise and strategic vision. This is very similar to the example I gave in chapter 4 with the doctor and the surgeon.

In most cases, the compensation of a coach is directly proportional to the impact of their advice. If the coach has financial expertise and saves a company 20 percent on $10,000,000 in manufacturing costs, their value is $2,000,000. While they are more likely to make 10 percent of those savings, the $2,000,000 value they bring to the organization is *much* higher than someone managing their website or SEO (i.e., a freelancer) would bring.

We went through this transition at Foley Media, and it helped us quadruple our monthly revenue by focusing on value instead of billing hourly. We also focused on solving more relevant problems.

As I mentioned in chapter 5, one of the biggest realizations I had with Foley Media was that there is a difference between tactics and strategy. Most of our clients wanted to buy a tactic, like SEO, but they lacked a cohesive digital strategy. Sure, we could help with individual tactics, but if they were not tied together, they were unlikely to get results.

For the most part, the reason people were buying individual tactics was a matter of understanding; they were simply telling us what they knew and thought they needed. We started testing more education and strategy work before doing anything tactical. As a result, our revenues skyrocketed because we were making bigger impacts on our customers' businesses.

This shift from freelancing in web development and SEO to education and strategy allowed us to talk to more senior stakeholders and work on higher-value projects.

Like I said, the value you provide is crucial because it relates to compensation. The more value you provide, the more you can charge. Once you understand the value you bring, you can comfortably and confidently raise your rates. If I am able to generate a ninety-times return for a client, they are much more likely to pay me two or three times what they'd pay my competition.

Coaching and consulting is the single best way to deliver your value for an immediate return. It also has the shortest path to success. When I changed Foley Media to be more consulting-based, we quadrupled our monthly retainer revenues. Since then we've continued to see double-digit growth monthly. It came down to two things:

1. Charging what we were worth
2. Focusing on what we were good at (and letting the rest go)

6.6. Scared to Start?

If you find yourself spinning your wheels and getting caught in false start mode, or wasting time on a logo, business cards, and a website, it is likely because you're hiding from your fears.

I remember when my first client agreed to pay me, I was in a state of shock. I called everyone close to me, including my mom, who had no clue why someone would pay me to get their business on Google.

I remember quickly going from excitement to panic.

There have been countless times since starting Foley Media when I doubted myself and wanted to quit. I wondered if I was really an expert and worthy of asking people for money! Those feelings are all completely normal, which is why we covered imposter syndrome in chapter 4. Living on that edge of doubt is what pushes you to learn and grow.

My discomfort forced me to learn. Every time I hit a roadblock or began to feel that "not-good-enough-ness," I read, watched videos, invested in training, and listened to audiobooks. When you get comfortable, you get complacent.

Every single person reading this book is an expert at something, and there is someone out there who needs their expertise. Here are some examples from *The Happiness of Pursuit Podcast* of odd passions that turned into lifestyle careers:

- Reading Classic Literature for Amazon
- Tagging Sharks for Wildlife Research
- Professional Photography for Business Portraits

- Online Training for Pharmacists
- Golf Influencer Turned Golf Channel Host
- Lawyer Turned PR Agency Owner

There's no shortage of ideas. The challenge is aligning your unique talents and expertise to the problems your market has and having the courage to ask for compensation.

In this section, I helped you build the foundation of your lifestyle business and your Breakout Blueprint. But foundations are not enough—I need to show you how to start building your business.

Now, it's time to help you put your Breakout Blueprint to work and make your lifestyle business a reality. In the following section, I am going to show you the steps to landing your first client, and how to avoid spending thousands of dollars over many frustrating months.

If you're ready to take the next step toward living life on your own terms, keep reading.

Part III

Building Out Your Breakout Blueprint in the Real World

Chapter 7

False Starts—How to *Really* Begin Your Lifestyle Business

Until you have a paying customer, all you have is an idea.

If you Google "how to start a business," you will be inundated with listicles like "The Complete, 12-Step Guide to Starting a Business," which are based on institutional advice. Almost every one of those lists will have two things in it: a business plan and some type of financing.

The truth about most business advice (especially the free kind) is that it is rarely the advice most successful people followed. If you were to ask ten successful business owners in your community how many of them had a business plan when they started, I wouldn't be shocked if the answer were zero.

Business plans are an excuse to not get started and to borrow money. If anything, you should be able to put your business plan on one page; otherwise, it is too complicated to execute (especially when you are just getting started). Yes, that's a bold statement and goes against most of what people are taught in school about building a business, but these days, it is much faster to test before you invest.

Simply put, before you put the time, money, and effort into building a business, find your first customer. This applies to online courses as much as it does to physical products. It is why there is a rise in crowdfunding campaigns. People can now reach out to the crowd, help solve a problem, and get funding to build the product once demand is proven. Ten years ago, companies would do market research and gamble on whether they got it right or not.

In the previous chapter, I walked you through a number of examples of businesses, from training to physical products to coaching. Now I am going to dive deeper into what those business models actually look like and how to build the lifestyle business you really want.

The reason this step is so important is that, if you do it wrong, you will create another job for yourself, rather than a vehicle to accomplish your life's mission. For example, do you want to be tied to an office every day, or do you want the freedom to work remotely? Do you want to work regularly structured hours while your kids are in school, or work evenings as a side hustle? Perhaps you want to work in project sprints, taking mini-retirements. The advantage of entrepreneurship is you have the freedom to choose.

Remember, as your business grows, you may elect to incorporate additional models for added revenue streams, but when you start it is important to pick one and go! You are not fixed in your business model, but I encourage you to think carefully about how to align your business with what you want your life to look like and what gives you the most fulfillment, because business is hard!

7.1. Business Models

7.1.1. Product-Based versus Service-Based

If you want to make $100,000 a year, all you have to do is charge $50/hour and work a full week. If you want to make that working part-time (say twenty hours per week), all you have to do is charge $100/hour. If you want to make that only working half of the year, all you need to do is figure out how to make $5,000 per week.

Below I am going to compare some of the most common

operating models for building a business, and more specifically the ones that cater toward building a lifestyle business that enables you to live life on your own terms.

7.2. Product Models

7.2.1. Digital Products versus Physical Products

When I was working at a content agency, we regularly used to tell clients to use the COPE methodology when creating content. COPE stands for Create Once, Publish Everywhere.

This is the difference between digital and physical products. Whereas you create a piece of online content once and publish it everywhere, a physical product constantly requires production, distribution, and sales.

Product-related businesses have their place, but they aren't likely to become lifestyle businesses simply because they require too much work and structure.

7.2.2. Service-Based Business versus Product-Based Business

The price you charge for a product or service is directly related to value the buyer perceives. In most cases, the bigger the problem, the higher the price of the solution.

In most industries, products have been killed by procurement departments. They look at products as widgets and try to find a way to commoditize them. While certain companies have done a great job at protecting their ideas via patents or copyrights, at the end of the day, any product can and will be knocked off, which devalues it.

In addition to the slow devaluation of products, you have higher staffing requirements for designing the product, testing it, producing it, managing the inventory, sales, markdowns of overstock, distribution, returns, etc. No matter how you try to do it—even as a "drop shipper" (someone who tries to spot a trend, creates demand online, and has a third party ship direct to a customer)— managing physical products is very labor-intensive.

Service-based businesses, on the other hand, require a lot less labor and often lean on the expertise an individual has to offer. In most cases, these are run by consultants, or solopreneurs. Service-based businesses are taking up an increasingly large proportion of the workforce as we transition to the "gig economy" and see an increase in skilled trades (the ultimate version of service-based businesses).

A plumber, electrician, or gas fitter is required to go through specific schooling to hone their craft. When someone has a leak, is about to do a home renovation, or wants to build a house, they require services that only these experts can perform.

What this means is that we are placing a higher value on experts who solve problems. Thus, the more hyper-knowledgeable you are in a given area, the higher you can charge. While you may not have gone to school for a dedicated trade, you have picked up a specific skillset during your career, which, when packaged correctly, can provide significant value to a defined audience.

Now, in any given service industry, there are huge variations in price. If you ask three plumbers to quote a bathroom renovation, you're likely going to get three very different prices. One will just get it done, one will provide some additional quality, and one will give you the luxury spa you've been dying for.

What you choose to buy is directly related to what you value.

The same is true in consulting and freelancing. When you are starting, you will underprice yourself. Remember how when I first started I charged my first client $375 per month? As I've gained more experience and brought more value to the audiences I serve, that rate has increased tenfold. There are times when I am paid $5,000 a day to speak or train at conferences.

The challenge I ran into was that I was limited by the time I had to consult and meet client deliverables, and there was a ceiling on how much people were willing to pay. Plus, I was becoming consumed by the work and no longer able to enjoy my reason for creating a business in the first place—time and financial freedom. I was living life not on my own terms, but on those of my clients.

That forced me to rebuild my model into something I call "The Solution Model." This allowed me to meet each level of the market with relevant helpful tools and reserve my time and energy for consulting clients without getting burnt out.

7.2.3. The Solution Model

We know that digital products give you the most freedom, but they often target the lower end of the market, and high-ticket consulting often consumes a lot of time. To balance these three things, I rebuilt my entire delivery process by taking what I learned from observing hundreds of other entrepreneurs and applying their models to a different industry.

I had three types of customers: those who wanted training and advice, those who wanted to be told what to do, and those who wanted me to do everything for them. In more simple terms—and this is applicable to every industry—people who wanted to do it themselves (DIY, do it yourself), people who wanted help doing it (DWY, done with you), and people who wanted it done for them (DFY, done for you).

The more involved we were, the more we charged, and the better the results were.

- For the DIY clients, we partnered with a company to do online training and offered half-day and full-day lessons.
- For the DWY clients, we offered half-day and full-day strategy sessions, as well as a mentorship program that included the online training.
- Finally, for the DFY clients, we offered a three-month strategy program and retainer services. These also included the mentorship program and online training.

What made this effective was that it allowed our clients to ascend to the next level as their businesses grew, while maintaining profitability by automating the delivery at lower levels and freeing up our time to give an amazing client experience to those who valued our expertise.

7.3. Lifestyle Fit

So why did I create the solution model? It came down to something very simple. I reread the Steve Jobs quote from his 2005 Stanford Commencement speech:

"For the past thirty-three years, I have looked in the mirror and asked myself: 'If today were the last day of my life, would I want to do what I'm about to do?' And whenever the answer has been 'No' for too many days in a row, I know I need to change something."

About six years after creating Foley Media, I realized I had built a trap. I was stuck in a new job, and it took me almost three years to break free and realize that I could build a more efficient model. As you begin to build your model, I encourage you to revisit chapter 2 and ask yourself what you want your ideal day, week, month, and year to look like. It will prevent you from getting trapped in the rat race again and give you clarity to focus on the bigger picture.

REMEMBER: This is a journey. Nothing you decide today is set in stone. As you grow and evolve, so can your decisions. You are not bound by the business model you choose while reading this book. You can always refer back to the previous chapters later down the line and go through the exercises to determine if your business model is still the right fit for you.

As you begin this journey, I can promise you that your Facebook and Instagram feeds are going to be destroyed by sponsored ads with webinars and courses offering to teach you "how to build a 7-figure funnel" or "how to create evergreen cashflow with digital courses." There is nothing more absurd than people selling courses about selling a course about building a course to sell courses...

Don't be that business. Just learn from those businesses and understand how they created their own Breakout Blueprints and leverage of digital versus physical product models. Each model has its benefits, but the most important thing to understand is how your model aligns with the business and lifestyle you want, and how it aligns with the customer's expectations.

7.4. How to Begin

"If you build it, they will come..."

—FIELD OF DREAMS

Many Foley Media clients have come to us after failed launches of online training programs. Companies spend thousands of dollars developing courses that will "change lives" in the hopes of finding an evergreen stream of online revenues. Then when they launch, they don't get any sales.

So what did they do? They purchased a course about "how to launch your online course." They implemented what they learned and made a couple of sales, but nothing near what they put into building the course. So what do they do *next?* Hire a coach! That coach gives them an entirely new strategy on "how to launch an online coaching program."

Here's the problem—in every case, they were focused on themselves! They didn't look at the product and ask: "Is it solving the right problem for the right audience at the right time?"

As one of my mentors, Oli Billson, told me: "It's a lot easier to sell pain pills than it is to sell vitamins...People are more likely to take out their wallet for an opportunity to change their life (pain pills) than for slow, gradual improvements (vitamins)."

Instead of wasting countless hours and thousands of dollars building something, just find someone with a problem, tell them you can solve it, and ask for payment— then go work like crazy to build your business! This is why I had you go through the exercises in chapters 5 and 6 to understand the needs of your market. Before you proceed, pull out those notes and pick one *problem* and one *solution*. This is the key here: identifying a problem that you can step in and solve. And if you can solve it and be paid for it, you may have a business. This will be our first test to see if your business has legs.

This is a lesson I hold true to this day: sell it first, build it second!

7.5. Validating Your Idea

If you are trying to climb a mountain or run a marathon, you need to start moving toward the summit. Building a business works exactly the same way, and if you want to build the best possible version of your business, the first thing you need to do is find someone who will pay for your services.

This is something Tim Ferriss refers to as the "Pay Certainty Test." It's one of the most profound lessons from *The 4-Hour Workweek*, which I highly suggest reading once you finish this book. I shared the basics of this principle in the introduction of this chapter, but here's the full story.

Ferriss derived this principle while figuring out how to validate his T-shirt company idea. Tim built a very simple website, purchased some Google ads, and had potential customers navigate all the way through the website, and he even allowed them to click "purchase." But instead of processing the transaction, he sent them to the "Out of Stock" page.

Once he reached one hundred purchases, he knew his business idea was likely worth pursuing.

As I move through this chapter, I will show you how to validate your product or service. It all starts with finding your first customer.

7.6. How to Find Your First Customer

For most people, asking for a sale is terrifying, so start with your family and then your friends and past colleagues. This is a technique that helped my friend Robyn when she was struggling to choose between two business ideas. Her first idea was an online education business to show people how to build an auction company; the second was a service-based business for female entrepreneurs.

Robyn and I met at a mastermind about a year earlier. At the time, she had a passion for helping women, but really wanted to see the online auction training company through. During the year we had connected a few times and I could tell her passion for supporting female entrepreneurs was growing. One day I got a text from Robyn that read, "Do you have 7 mins this morning to talk? I'd love to bounce something off you?"

We chatted for fifteen minutes about which idea she should start with, the auction program or the service for female entrepreneurs. I asked her a simple question, "In all of your years selling to other women, how many connections do you have that you could text to get their opinion?"

Robyn quickly replied, "A thousand!"

That was all she needed. At 10:28 a.m. I challenged her to text ten people right away with the following script:

"Morning {name}, I'm launching a marketing foundations program for 'her.'

I'm looking for 10 people who I admire to be part of the beta group to provide feedback as I build out the program. When the program launches it will be $1,000...but for the initial 10 it will only be $100 (my way of saying thanks for the feedback).

Let me know if you are interested and I'll send more details."

At 10:51 a.m. I received the following text from Robyn: "Wowsers!!! That was the scariest, most accelerating thing I've done (in a long time)...and before I could send the 10th text I got 2 YES's and 2 requests for more details back..."

While one could argue it took Robyn a year to lock in her first customer, this approach will help accelerate your timeline and get you the feedback you need to get started and potentially land your first paying client.

To make it easier, here is a simple template you can use to do some outreach:

"Hi {name},

I recently decided to start a business helping {insert customer type} to {insert primary problem} by {insert solution}.

Version one: I am reaching out to you as a (friend/family/colleague/potential customer) to see if you, or anyone that you know, would benefit from this service?

Version two: I am reaching out to you as a (friend/family/colleague/potential customer) to get your feedback on the idea.

Thank you,

{Your name}"

The point of this exercise is to get a quick win. Find a customer, find out what they would be willing to pay, and start! As simple as it sounds, most people NEVER get started because they spend all of their time studying their potential market and puzzling over the dreaded false start question: "Will it scale?" This question can be essential when it comes to product businesses because you need more demand to validate production (which is what Tim Ferriss faced in running his T-shirt business). For service-based businesses, however, when you start, you are trying to go from one customer to ten, then ten to one hundred. In doing the work, you will get to understand your customer, solve more important problems, and develop new higher-value skills, and as a result you'll be able to charge more.

With all that said, avoiding false starts is crucial to helping you keep up your momentum.

7.7. Avoiding False Starts

What is a false start?

According to Lexico, a false start is "an invalid or disallowed start to a race, usually due to a competitor beginning before the official signal has been given."[*] In sports, false starts lead to penalties or, depending on the sport and how many false starts are already accumulated, disqualification.

Why do athletes false start? Mostly due to anxiety. False starts are common in sports like swimming and running, where a fraction of a second can make a difference—this puts pressure on an athlete and can lead to a false start.

False starts are common in business as well. There's so much anxiety around trying to make it as an entrepreneur, people reach for any and all advice they can find. And as we discussed at the beginning of this chapter, so many people have been misguided by traditional and, quite frankly, bad advice.

- Get a domain.
- Build a website.
- Design a logo.
- Print business cards.
- Register as a corporation.

---

[*] https://www.lexico.com/en/definition/false_start.

- Get a phone number.
- Hire a VA.
- Write a business plan.
- Get a bank account.

Stop it. You don't have a business unless you have customers, and all of these things mentioned above are false-start activities. Don't do them. Instead, figure out the problem you can solve for a defined audience, what they are willing to pay (the value), and then go get your first customer!

Here's an example of how Mitch Atkins avoided a false start by creating a Minimum Viable Product and getting a paying customer, all while pursuing his dream of playing professional hockey.

A few years ago, Mitch called me to ask if we could grab a coffee because he was trying to figure out how to land an internship in marketing. When we met, I asked Mitch why he wanted a marketing internship. His answer, like that of most soon-to-be college grads, was: "I want work experience that would look good on my resume, and I want to know how business really works."

I followed that up with one more simple question: "What do you want to do after college?" and he replied, "Play professional hockey."

There was no value in Mitch getting an internship, so I gave him this simple challenge: "Why don't you start your own business?" (I thought his mother, a close friend, was going to kill me after I gave that advice.) After flushing out his business on the back of a napkin, I gave him one simple challenge, and it is the same task I would ask all of you to complete after finishing this chapter:

Go find one paying client before you do ANYTHING else. No business cards, no website, no logo. Just a value-added service that someone pays you for (yes, cash in hand).

Mitch went from $0 to $5,000 in his first summer (he built this business while he was still in school) and has continued to scale, enabling him to play professional hockey in the minor leagues. And we're going to explore how he did it.

If you're reading this book, you are probably full of ideas. The problem is choosing one and getting started. In the previous chapter, you put down three to five ideas that you could use to create a business. Here is a process you can follow to see *which* idea is the one to start with.

One of the worst things you can do is go broad. Do NOT try to solve all of your clients' problems with a massive service. Pick one and own it! Think of it this way: the more you specialize, the more value you bring to a client, and the more they are willing to pay. To help make this process easier, I am going to walk through how Mitch and I narrowed down his service offering during our coffee chat.

In Mitch's case, he had a pretty good understanding of the problem he wanted to solve: the pain felt by undrafted hockey players. He knew this pain well because he was an undrafted hockey player himself. He wanted to play at a higher level but was not drafted by an NHL team. Fortunately, he found a way to continue playing hockey. Because the NHL draft happens pre-college, he was able to reach out to NCAA hockey programs and eventually land a scholarship at Elmira College. Mitch could have thrown in the towel and ended his hockey career early, but his perseverance helped him get an education and propelled him to a professional career in hockey after college.

His experience was similar to what so many junior hockey players go through. In hearing his story, I shared with him that what he had done for himself, he could do for so many others.

We looked at three options:

- An online course
- A membership community
- Consulting/coaching

Based on our mutual experience with the recruiting process, we quickly identified the consulting and coaching path as the fastest win with the most value. Mitch had a network of players and coaches he could reach out to immediately to validate the idea—which is what he did.

A junior hockey team invited Mitch to speak about his experience and educate players about the opportunity to play in the NCAA. That gave him a reason to develop a website and a simple brand, so that he could offer something at the end of the presentation.

One of the most important things in business is getting early quick wins. There is nothing more powerful than building momentum. Consulting would allow Mitch to share his expertise on day one without having to first build an expensive and time-consuming infrastructure. He could spend his time learning from clients and reinvesting profits, instead of accumulating debt to get started.

Robyn and Mitch got results because they followed the process. They knew how they wanted to help and then just asked for clients. They didn't get stuck making false starts—they simply went to work!

If you're ready to put in the work, keep reading and I will show you how to go from landing that first client to building something that provides true freedom.

Chapter 8

Transforming Your Side Hustle into a Business That Gives You True Freedom

"Oh shit, they said yes!"

You've found your first client and they've said yes! Now you feel like the dog who caught the car and isn't sure what to do next. I was in the same boat nine years ago when I landed my first client. I had no idea how to formulate my offering. I just had a skill that I could use to help them grow.

What I didn't realize until close to six years in is that growing a business takes a lot more than just your skillset. It takes a ton of time, patience, and stamina. It will test your willpower, your relationships, and your sanity. And at some point, you are going to have to make some tough decisions and some hard sacrifices. In the last chapter, we talked about how to get started by finding your first customer. Now we're going to go over what it takes to make your business a business: to transform your side hustle into something that offers you true freedom.

8.1. Burning the Boats: Going All In

We begin with the simple lesson of "burning the boats." It's a Julius Caesar quote: "If you want to take the island, you need to burn the boats." This is how Caesar instructed his army in battle. When they got to the shores, they would burn their boats. This was a powerful statement to the enemy because it told them the Roman army was going to win or die trying.

When you take away your source of retreat, your only option is success. This means you need to go all in. It took me seven years of struggling to finally go all in. Once I did that, it only took me nine months to go from earning a few thousand dollars per month to making over six figures. That's the commitment and drive it takes to transform your side hustle into your lifestyle business.

But CAUTION! This is not an invitation to accumulate

thousands of dollars in credit card debt, make reckless decisions, or borrow money from your family. You need to be prepared to build your business within your own means. Don't quit your job tomorrow—it took me almost seven years to be able to do that. Take Julius Caesar's quote to heart, but know that there's a difference between burning the boats once you are on the shore and lighting them on fire when you're in the middle of the ocean!

I'll tackle this in more detail later. For now, let's explore how I turned my side hustle into a full-time business. It comes down to income versus impact.

8.2. Income versus Impact

You've just landed your first client. Almost every interviewee on *The Happiness of Pursuit* remembers their first sale, and the majority had that moment of "Oh shit, now what?" This is totally normal. I still get that feeling when I sign clients, but we have developed processes that manage those "oh shit" moments so that they aren't emotional roller coasters.

Your first client is going to shape the future of your business. Chances are, if you are anything like me or most people starting a business, you are going to completely undervalue yourself.

After landing my first client, I would work hours upon hours making sure I got amazing results for them. I didn't have kids then, so it was easy to put in eight to ten hours at my day job, then come home and put in another five to eight hours figuring out how to service my client.

The problem, which I wouldn't realize for almost two years, was that I was working for about $4/hour. Because I had underpriced myself, I didn't leave room for growth, which was an easy mistake to make because my full-time job was covering the bills and the money I made independently was almost "play money" to fund my entrepreneurial education.

As I gained confidence, I was able to raise my rates and outsource some of the work. Still, the money coming in wasn't enough for me to leave my job anytime soon. The overwhelming question of "Do I go all in, or do I pack it in?" was alive and well!

I had to make a very conscious decision that if I was going to make this happen—if I was going to "burn the boats"—I would have to charge ten times what I was charging.

I will never forget the moment when I sent the proposal for $1,500 per month for twelve months and three weeks later for $3,500 per month for six months; now I have six-figure consulting clients. The moment you see your true value—*that* is the moment you become unstoppable (as long as you stay humble).

If you can help a business double, triple, or even quadruple their revenues, they will pay proportionately. In certain circumstances, you may even solve some problems that go beyond business. You may give time back to a business owner by implementing systems that enable them to do the things they love, like coaching their child's Little League team.

I stopped seeing money as a way to fill my selfish need for "things" and instead looked at it as jet fuel for my business. I reinvested in myself and went to more conferences, took online courses, purchased competitive products to see how they worked, and, most importantly, surrounded myself with amazing people who were years ahead of where I was on my journey.

I realized if I could find a way to provide value to people, I could compound my impact and gain success and fulfillment.

That decision allowed me to build a team and expand my ability to change businesses. It gave me the clarity I needed for my mission to help a thousand people build lifestyle businesses—whether through this book, through *The Happiness of Pursuit*, or through our clients at Foley Media.

8.3. Lifestyle Design: Building a Truly Free Business

In the introduction, I talked to you about building a business that would give you freedom to focus on the important things in your life. This is crucial because entrepreneurship can often be a hustle. So much of a hustle, in fact, that you never *stop* hustling. At times it is a flat-out wear-you-down-to-the-bone grind.

I know it was like that for me. Before I realized the difference between an income mindset and an impact mindset, I was trying to do it ALL: build a business; be a good father, husband, and brother; keep a single-digit handicap; run a podcast; write a book; *and* work. There just weren't enough hours in a day to do it all, at least not well.

Once I started focusing on my value and aligning my rates with the kind of life I wanted to live, my business became an enterprise that helped me live a more enriching life. I could take my dad to The Masters for his eightieth birthday, take trips with my wife, have weekly date nights, and have more quality time with my kids. It wasn't about the extravagant things. It was about having the financial means to enjoy time with the people I loved the most.

That is why lifestyle design matters. As you transform your side hustle into your main business, it is vital for you to know what type of life you want, so that the business you build supports it.

So, what does lifestyle design really look like?

Is there a family vacation you went on as a kid that brings back a warm feeling every time you think about it—something you want to replicate again and again? It is likely similar to how you feel about the ideal day you built in chapter 2.

Lifestyle design is about trying to build your life around that feeling. It is about building a business that gives you the means to live life on your own terms. If you want to work four hours per week and make $100,000 a year, it is possible! It just means you have to charge $481/hour. Yes—just $481/hour ($481 × 4 = $1,924 × 52 = $100,048).

Here's the path to $100,000 a few different ways:

Working hourly full-time = $50/hour [$100,000/2,000 working hours]

Four-hour work week = $481/hour [$100,000/(52 × 4)]

Daily = $274 [$100,000/365]

Weekly = $1,924 [$100,000/52]

Monthly = $8,334 [$100,000/12]

As the unit of time increases, it looks like a more challenging task, but if I told you all you had to do to leave your full-time job was sell $2,000 worth of a digital product or consulting service, would you be willing to do it?

That's four clients at $500 a month. Do you know four people for whom you could do a $500 task in one or two hours? If so, working eight to ten hours a month, you could make over $100,000 a year. Of course, there are taxes and other expenses that may come with that, but the important thing is getting past the fear that you're not good enough to make the salary you want! You have a skill that's worth $500 to someone. Chances are you have one that's worth $1,000 or more! Have the courage to go after the life you want and make space for the things that matter. Put lifestyle design at the center of your thinking about your business. Trust me, it matters.

8.4. Side Hustle versus All In

So you're ready to go all in? Before you do, here are some serious things to consider.

When I got serious about building my business, I learned

how much harder it was than I thought it would be. As you grow your business you are going to encounter unforeseen problems. To help you through those times, it's important to have capital, comfort, and financial security. That means not making the jump until you're *ready* to make it—no matter how long that may take.

When people ask me if I wish I'd started building my business sooner, I would like to say yes. But in reality, it would have likely meant financial ruin. Remember: burn the boats on the shore, not in the middle of the ocean! When you are starting your business, you must build a track record of six months of financial success—to be blunt, you need to be making money before you quit your day job. Growing a business without capital is one of the most stressful and life-sucking things you can do to yourself, your business, and your most important relationships.

Having just your basic bills covered will enable you to scale your business ten times faster than you could while using profits from your business to pay your mortgage or put food on the table. With the latter approach, you will quickly turn your ticket to freedom into a job and become a slave to this new machine.

The added advantage of having limited time to work on this side hustle is that it will force you to become more efficient. Recall your time in school: if you were anything like me, you would wait until the last minute to study for a big test or finish an assignment. This is all part of "Parkinson's Law," which according to Lexico is "the notion that work expands so as to fill the time available for its completion."*

If you look at the time you make available—and what I really mean is the time to which you limit yourself—you have an opportunity to build your business while only working the hours you want. You can find a way to build a business where you work fifteen to twenty hours per week to align with your lifestyle design. The constraints become the blueprint for what you want your business to look like.

Now, let's take a look at your goals and figure out how to achieve them more efficiently. When it comes to setting goals for your lifestyle business, I need to get clear on three things:

- Revenue—How much do you need/want to make?
- Time—How much do you want to work? How much are you willing to work?
- Reward—What are you going to do when you reach that goal?

While this is the least scientific method of goal setting,

* https://www.lexico.com/definition/parkinson's_law

it will give you the foundation you need when you ask yourself, "Am I ready to burn the boats?" Below, we're going to dive into each of these points. In each section, I've mentioned additional resources. I encourage you to look to them for more examples of goal setting and for the tools I use to stay on track.

8.4.1. Revenue Goals

There are two very important numbers you need to consider when you develop your revenue goals:

1. How much money you need to live without sacrificing your current lifestyle
2. How much money you want in order to live your ideal life

If you want to know how to calculate both of these, I would read the blog post on "Ideal Lifestyle Costing" by Tim Ferriss (tim.blog/lifestyle-costing/), as well as the section about Dream Lining with the expense calculator: tim.blog/expense-calculator/.

8.4.2. Time Commitment

If you have been interested in "entrepreneurship" for a while, you have probably seen thousands of posts of wannabe entrepreneurs standing in front of Ferraris, on private jets, or taking luxury vacations. "Entrepreneurship" has become a buzzword associated with luxury and the hustle.

The truth is, entrepreneurship is more about freedom and living life on your own terms. If you want to work fifteen hours per week, then do it! But first, figure out what you need to get to your goals and whether or not you are willing to put in the work.

I'll use the example of running a marathon, which is probably the best metaphor for what building a successful and sustainable business is really like.

Everyone can run a marathon, whether they're a three-year-old or an eighty-three-year-old. *And* they can do it without any training. Now you are probably thinking, "That's impossible," but remember: a marathon is strictly a matter of distance. If you decide that the marathon needs to be completed within a certain time frame, however, then that requires more effort than a three-year-old and an eighty-three-year-old are likely capable of.

In life and business, the same rules apply. We have the opportunity to choose what our time frame is, which will dictate how much effort we need to put into getting there.

For example, if you want to build a million-dollar business, what you do on a daily basis depends on if your goal is to create it over ten years or over the next six months.

So many business owners get caught up in the aura of a "seven-figure business," but many who have made it to that point were much happier in the mid-to-upper six figures. One thing I can tell you is that no matter which target you choose, the time it takes to get there is often twice as long, and the work twice as hard, as you imagine.

The reason why comes down to lack of knowledge. You don't know what you don't know, and learning takes time and money. Plus, what you do for your first customer will be different from what you do with your tenth customer, because you get better at your craft over time. You will find better ways to do things, including some things you absolutely hate doing. Think of it as going through business puberty. That awkward stage of figuring out who you are is difficult, but we all make it through.

It's easy to get overly excited about how soon you'll be flying in private jets, but understand there is a lot to learn and there will be growing pains along the way.

When you first start, your time is going to be divided among three things: finding clients, winning their business, and keeping their business. More simply put, 30 percent of your time will be spent on sales-related activities, like networking, prospecting, and eventually marketing and advertising. Thirty percent of your time will be spent on meetings, proposals, contracts, and pitching to prospects. And finally, 60 percent of your time will be spent on fulfilling the work and keeping clients happy.

Now you're probably thinking: "Wait a minute! Thirty percent plus 30 percent plus 60 percent is 120 percent of my time." I will make one a simple promise to you—when you first start this exercise, you will spend twice as much time as you think servicing your clients. Make sure you budget and time block accordingly.

So, if you plan to work twenty hours per week, save an extra four hours for getting caught up. Not doing this is one giant mistake I made early, which meant a lot of late nights—this is why so many entrepreneurs have to "hustle": simply because they didn't plan.

Finally, if you really want to make sure you are using your time effectively, schedule it and track it! The following exercise will keep you honest and help you make adjustments. You are going to make mistakes and have to research solutions or find partners. This is all part of the entrepreneur's journey to mastery.

8.4.3. Reward

There is nothing more gratifying to a runner than crossing the finish line at the end of a marathon. But if you ask them what it felt like *during* the process, they'll say it was pure hell and only the joy of finishing made it worthwhile. So how do so many people finish? They have checkpoints and mile markers so they can see their progress!

You need to do the same thing for your business. Create micro-rewards for each milestone and larger rewards for the big ones. This is the exact process I used to make sure I finished this book, and the one I use to celebrate new client wins for our agency.

The goal for this book was to write 250 words per day, which works out to approximately one page. Some days I was able to write more than two thousand words. Other days I struggled to get through 250. Those small steps helped me make progress. The mile markers, and times we celebrated, were for bigger steps, like finishing my rough draft, submitting my manuscript, or choosing a cover design.

Whenever our agency and consulting practice signed a client, my wife and I would have a glass of wine or, my personal favorite, a glass of Blanton's Bourbon.

Just like finishing a marathon, the discipline of putting

one foot in front of the other is what gets your business to succeed. Find daily, weekly, and monthly rewards, along with incentives when you reach different milestones, and never forget to celebrate. When you stop celebrating the wins, it is a sign that you might need to reevaluate the business.

8.5. Are You Ready, Willing, and Able?

Now that you know what it takes to build your lifestyle business, I want you to take a good, hard look in the mirror and ask yourself: "Am I willing to make this commitment?"

I have seen so many great ideas fail for one simple reason—the people didn't want it bad enough. When you look at your goal worksheet, it is going to seem overwhelming. This is when most people throw in the towel, or make an even worse mistake and work on nonessential tasks like branding and website-building.

Be honest with yourself! Are you going to do the work that's necessary to build and grow a business? If you can commit to what's on your goal sheet and build good habits, I promise you that your lifestyle business will change your life.

Chapter 9

Conclusion

"You know, sometimes all you need is twenty seconds of insane courage. Just literally twenty seconds of just embarrassing bravery. And I promise you, something great will come of it."

—BENJAMIN MEE, *WE BOUGHT A ZOO*

Benjamin Mee and his family acted on their passion for wildlife—they bought a zoo. They made their dream a reality. While I'm not telling you to "bet the farm" (or in this case "the zoo"), I want you to believe that you can leverage the Breakout Blueprint to build the life you want to live.

With the Breakout Blueprint, you have what you need to exit the corporate life and begin living on your own terms. I have shown you through my own experiences and advice from the guests of my podcast what is possible.

I can promise you that as you embark on your own journey, you will have doubts about yourself as an entrepreneur, your ability to serve your customers, and your ability to juggle family, business, and the life experiences you want—it is all normal! Take time to enjoy the journey and learn at each and every step.

As I said, the reason I called my podcast *The Happiness of Pursuit* is simple—it is in the journey of life, and in doing the things that we love, that we find lasting happiness and fulfillment. If you're constantly chasing it, you will never be present enough to find it or enjoy it.

Surround yourself with people you aspire to be like, and if I can help you along that journey, please feel free to reach out to me on social media using @douglasjfoley. Build out your network and support structure with people who will "kick your ass if you don't pursue this..."—like Paul did for me.

I want to leave you with this thought from Dr. Seuss:

"You have brains in your head. You have feet in your shoes. You can steer yourself any direction you choose. You're on your own. And you know what you know. And YOU are the one who'll decide where to go..."

—DR. SEUSS, *OH, THE PLACES YOU'LL GO!*

I wish you nothing but wild success! Enjoy the journey, my friends.

Acknowledgments

This book would not have been possible without the love, support, and immense patience of my wife, Carrie. Thank you for pushing me, picking me up when I was down, and challenging me to look in the mirror when I needed to find a better path!

To my children, Hunter and Harper, while it will be a while before you read and understand this, I want to thank you for making me grow up while staying young. You have taught me so much in such a short time. I want this book to guide you to live a fulfilling life.

To my parents, as long as I can remember you've given me the freedom to fail, the courage to try, and the knowledge that no matter what, I had a family who loved me, something I want my children to grow up knowing too.

To my brothers (by birth and by circumstance), you blazed a trail that made it so much easier for me to become an entrepreneur. You shared what life was really like. You gave me opportunities to work with you side by side. You coached me through tough decisions, and definitely let me know when I made bad ones. You've always been there when I needed help and to help me celebrate.

To my sisters, thank you for believing in me. No matter what I was trying to do, you had my back without question. You always helped me see the gentler side of life. Your love means the world to me.

To Paul, you pushed me outside my comfort zone to take a risk on myself (well, actually you told me you'd kick my ass and I believed you!). Everyone needs to find a "Paul" in their life to push them!

To my clients, this journey wouldn't have been possible without you. I have learned so much from working with all of you.

To my podcast guests, you gave me an opportunity to hear your wisdom and share it with the world. Every interview helped me better understand how much abundance there is in this world!

To Zach, Tucker, Hal, Ellie, Rachel, Tashan, and the entire

team at Scribe, you not only helped pull this book out of me, but through the process helped me better understand who I am as a husband, a father, a son, a brother, a friend, and an entrepreneur.

To all the listeners, followers, fans, and friends, every time you commented, shared, or sent a note of gratitude, it gave me fulfillment and the courage to continue. It was the small wins you shared that helped me get through this book and pushed me to carry on in this crazy pursuit.

About the Author

Doug Foley is a media entrepreneur, podcast host, and digital pioneer who is known for pushing the boundaries of digital platforms to create unique solutions that drive growth. He's an innovator with a drive and a passion for helping others thrive, succeed, and think outside the box.

As the host of the hit podcast *The Happiness of Pursuit*, he teaches listeners how ordinary people followed their passions to create extraordinary lives. He launched two six-figure agencies in less than eighteen months, and he's now using that experience to help others find fulfillment through lifestyle businesses.

CPSIA information can be obtained
at www.ICGtesting.com
Printed in the USA
BVHW042350050822
643900BV00017B/950/J